Public Speaking Handbook
for Librarians and Information Professionals

Public Speaking Handbook for Librarians and Information Professionals

SARAH R. STATZ

McFarland & Company, Inc., Publishers
Jefferson, North Carolina, and London

LIBRARY OF CONGRESS CATALOGUING-IN-PUBLICATION DATA

Statz, Sarah R., 1974–
Public speaking handbook for librarians and information professionals /
Sarah R. Statz.
p.   cm.
Includes bibliographical references and index.

ISBN 0-7864-1546-0 (softcover : 50# alkaline paper)∞

1. Communication in library science — Handbooks, manuals, etc.
2. Public speaking — Handbooks, manuals, etc.   I. Title.
Z716.3.S73   2003   808.5'1'088092 — dc21   2003009930

British Library cataloguing data are available

Cover photograph © 2003 Comstock Images

Manufactured in the United States of America

*McFarland & Company, Inc., Publishers
Box 611, Jefferson, North Carolina 28640
www.mcfarlandpub.com*

Contents

Part One. The Speaking Process

Part Two. The Speaking Environment

Introduction

One of the core competencies for librarians today is communication skills.
— Maggie Weaver, "Reach Out through Technology:
Make Your Point with Effective A/V"

"Can I have a copy of your script?"

Those eight short words were once the bane of my teaching-librarian existence. I remember hearing them after I taught workshops, during campus-wide bibliographic instruction "retreats," and at countless meetings held to address the challenges of teaching information literacy. The word "script" was pervasive and unavoidable. If your class went well, the other librarians wanted to see your script. If the library instruction coordinator's office heard good things about your presentation, they wanted to see a copy of your script. When you went to meetings to discuss library workshops, committees were appointed to write and distribute scripts. It should come as no surprise that, when I finally broke down and revealed my shameful secret, I was very nearly excommunicated from the ranks of the few, the proud, the public services and bibliographic instruction librarians.

I never had a script. And (this is the clever bit) you don't need one either.

I've confessed my secret to you because if you've read this far into a handbook on public speaking for librarians, it can be for one of only two reasons: either there's absolutely nothing else around to read, or (and I hope this is the one) you want to become a better public speaker. If that second one is indeed your reason, we have something in common. We share the belief that, as Peter Kenny put it in his public speaking handbook for engineers, "with a modest degree of study it is possible to improve one's public speaking ability" (Kenny 1982, 3). The only thing left to examine is, why do we want to improve our speaking ability?

The library profession is changing. When I say that, I don't mean technological changes (there will always be plenty of those, and they'll be heavily discussed in library research and journals); personnel changes (they're there too — more paraprofessionals and support staff than ever before keep libraries running smoothly); or even demographic

1

changes (that merely reflect the dynamic nature of our population and globalization in general). What I do mean is that librarians and information professionals can no longer be content to be the unseen collectors, classifiers, and guardians of information. We can't stop fulfilling those functions, but we must accept that telling our patrons about them, and publicizing them to our colleagues (both in the library and in our broader governing institutions) are an important part of doing them.

That assertion is echoed in the literature and statistics of our field. Cheryl LaGuardia, author of *Teaching the New Library*, has suggested that the "'new librarian' spheres of expertise include: intelligence, curiosity, empathy, and good interpersonal skills" (LaGuardia et al. 1996, 21). Michael Gordon Jackson, in *Advances in Librarianship*, argued that "Technical competency is not enough; there are other computer services experts on campus who can usually program and set up networks much better than librarians can ever hope to do" (Jackson 2000, 105). John Bertot and Charles McClure recently found that sixty-two percent of public libraries offer some kind of Internet training services to their patrons and to staff (Bertot and McClure 2000, 5). In addition to advertising our skills and teaching our patrons, we can't forget good old self-defense as motivation for bettering our speaking skills: librarian and author Anne Turner recognized that incentive when she stated that "Every staff person at every level, from book shelvers to the director, needs to have good communication skills to handle the problems they'll confront in the library world" (Turner 1993, 46).

So librarians and information professionals are doing more public speaking than ever before — at conferences, in meetings, when teaching classes or giving book talks, and in countless other situations. But are we doing it well, and more importantly, are we enjoying ourselves while doing so? At least one research study would indicate that we probably are not; Mary Jane Scherdin's fascinating 1992 study of 1,600 librarians who took the Myers-Briggs Type Indicator (MBTI) personality inventory found that "librarians are the opposite of the general population on Introversion and Intuition," and a whopping sixty-three percent of librarians display introverted tendencies (as compared to thirty-five percent in the general population) (Scherdin 1994, 105). What does that really mean? Fortunately, we can turn to the creators of the MBTI, Isabel Briggs Myers and Peter B. Myers, for their explanation of what it means to be an introvert: "Their dominant process is engrossed with the inner world of ideas, and the auxiliary process does what it can about their outer lives.... Most people see only the side introverts present to the outer world, which is mostly their auxiliary process, their second best" (Myers 1980, 12–13). Put another way (and this is the way that is discussed to death in library literature), many librarians are shy, and think that they have an image problem, which only makes them more shy. It's an ugly cycle, and it's one that would indicate that, although most people fear public speaking, librarians have even more reason to fear and dislike it.

It is my belief that our fear or dislike of public speaking is indicated not only by our obsession with our bookish and retiring image, but also by the complete and utter lack of any kind of resources addressing good speaking skills, written by us and for us. That void was noted by Danelle Hall (director of the Oklahoma City University Dulaney-Browne Library) as recently as May 2002: "It is perhaps significant that the past three years of Library Literature turned up only a handful of articles on the subject of public speaking, and those were in journals such as Searcher, Emedia, and Computer Librarian" (Hall 2002, 64).

There's bad news on several fronts; it appears that it's only going to become more important to develop good presentation skills, many librarians and information professionals may harbor introverted tendencies (which makes speaking in public even harder), and there aren't many articles or sources dedicated to the specialized challenges that librarians face when trying to improve their communication skills. All is not lost, however; "Introverts are usually better listeners than extroverts, since they are content to sit back and let the other person be the center of attention" (Hargie, Saunders, and Dixon 1994, 204). That should be heartening news, because many communications experts agree that good listening is the first step to good speaking. It might be scant consolation, but we can also depend on our library tradition for support: "The library system in the past functioned in a way that helped produce a century of social progress and technological innovation that is unmatched in the history of mankind. The reason for this success was not technology, although that certainly played a role, but relationships between people" (Bridges 2001, 54). If we could foster relationships among ourselves and others that served to promote progress and innovation, we can certainly apply a few basic speaking principles to our presentations that will promote the progress of all librarians and information professionals.

I offer this book only as the result of my speaking experiences and personal interest in the subject. I am not an expert speaker, or an expert researcher, or an expert writer. All I can promise you is that every time I stand before an audience, my stomach churns nervously, and my sole wish is to be somewhere else. Yet somehow, miraculously, while I'm speaking, exhilaration replaces the churning, and my wish to be away from my listeners becomes a desire to talk with them for much longer than I've been given. I'd like you to experience that too, not only because I think it's important for our skills base, and our presentations, and our audience, and our profession; but mainly because it's fun.

On second thought, perhaps I do have a copy of a script for you after all. It says, "Get out there and enjoy yourself, and your audience will enjoy themselves."

How This Book Is Organized

This book is divided into two parts. Part One offers basic principles for better speech preparation and delivery, and Part Two discusses the specific situations in which librarians often have to communicate. All professionals these days have many demands on their time, and library professionals are no different; therefore, the first six chapters are designed to be read and absorbed quickly, and offer general suggestions for creating, delivering, and evaluating a presentation from start to finish. The final five chapters are designed to be read as needed; for example, if you're currently in the process of job interviewing, you should consult Chapter 7 for ways to apply good public speaking techniques to your interview performances. Those same five chapters also include suggestions for further research on each subject; these are readings I found extremely helpful during the researching of this book, and are provided because finding and evaluating references regarding effective public speaking methods can be quite time-consuming.

At the very end of the book you will find an appendix containing five interviews with a variety of library and information professionals; I found conducting the interviews were the best part of researching this book, primarily because they prove in relatively short order that all speakers must develop their own style to be successful. You will also find two appendixes that are designed to take a little of the legwork out of finding helpful tips for using presentation software tools and reference resources that speakers can use to liven up their presentations or further develop their speaking style.

PART ONE
The Speaking Process

CHAPTER 1

Lend Me Your Ears

You can observe a lot just by watching.
— Yogi Berra, *I Really Didn't Say Everything I Said!*

Death and taxes may be the only two certainties in life, but if we're to believe the opinion polls most of us fear speaking in public more than either of those two certainties. Jerry Seinfeld illustrated the matter nicely when he stated that most of us would prefer to be in the casket at a funeral, rather than giving the eulogy.

The simple truth is that speaking in public is not easy, and the difficulty is compounded for those who fear it or do not count giving good speeches or presentations among their skills. How refreshing it should be, then, to learn that the first step toward becoming a good speaker is such an easy one: becoming a good listener.

To Become a Good Speaker, You Must First Become a Good Listener

Being a good listener is one of the most underrated skills in our profession. We are constantly bombarded by what we're told are the necessary competencies that will get us hired or promoted. We all know that we need to become as technologically literate as possible. We know that we need to work well with committees and teams. It is less often required that one of our competencies be the ability to listen, carefully and critically. Even encounters with patrons at the reference desk are referred to as the "reference interviews," giving the impression that we are there to grill people relentlessly, making them rephrase their questions until we finally understand what they're trying to ask. Thankfully, we don't carry the "interview" analogy to the point of asking our patrons where they hope to be in five years or what they think their weakest qualities are, but if we thought it might clarify their questions, I'm sure we would.

The strategies listed in this chapter are designed to help you step back and view your upcoming experience in the broader scheme of things; to help you realize that watching other speeches is a vital part of preparing your own (Menzel and Carrell 1994, 18). The strategies are intended to teach you the same critical listening skills that you will soon hope your future audiences exhibit as well.

Watch and listen to as many other speakers as possible

Our profession, like love, is a many-splendored thing. During any given week there are probably a number of opportunities for you to view presentations on a variety of subjects. At its most basic level, gaining an appreciation for how different people present different types of information can give you ideas on how to structure your own presentation. An informal book talk given by a public librarian will differ widely from an automation librarian's detailed discussion of the technical requirements of the new library catalog, and, although you may find one or the other more interesting to you personally, going to both helps you determine the best structure to use to approach your specific topic.

Contrary to popular belief, the ability to listen effectively is not innate. Experts conjecture that we spend most of our day listening to others at about twenty-five percent efficiency, and research on the subject has identified three levels of listening: level three, where we fake attention and spend most of our time "tuning out"; level two, where we hear the speaker's words but not his true intent; and level one, where we suspend judgment and listen empathetically to a speaker so as to understand her words and meaning (Burley-Allen 1995, 14). Unfortunately, there is a wide difference in how fast people can speak and how quickly they can hear: our average rate of speech is 125 to 175 words per minute, while our "thought rate," or how fast we can cognitively process what we hear, is a whopping 400 to 800 words per minute

(Hargie, Saunders, and Dickson 1994, 205). What are we supposed to do with all the extra time we have left on our hands after we've heard a speaker's words, other than fidget or daydream? Awareness of your listening behavior will enable you to follow some suggestions for becoming a better listener: listen for total meaning (as indicated through words and nonverbal communication and body language), listen with empathy (why does the speaker feel as he does, or from what point of view is he speaking?), and listen critically (how does the speaker support her viewpoint, or how did she arrive at the words and structure of the talk she is giving?).

If you don't have the opportunities (or the time) to observe more structured presentations or meetings, take the time to consider your daily personal interactions. Watch how your co-workers interact with one another and the library patrons. At home, listen carefully to the speech patterns and affectations of radio and television broadcasters; when shopping, note how salespeople approach you. One of the benefits of being a librarian is that we truly "work with the entire realm of the human family" (Manley 1992, 52). Because of that, we can train for our interactions with the public and each other by being attuned to the speech of that entire human family.

And watching others is one of the easiest and most beneficial ways to approach giving your own presentation. Not only will you get a break from your own job plus the chance to learn something new, but as you listen to different speakers, you will begin to see that effective presenters share certain characteristics, no matter what the subject. That is not to say that presentation styles are completely independent of the type of information being presented. It is merely an assertion that as you make an effort to listen to all speakers carefully, certain techniques and characteristics of "good" speaking will become apparent to you.

As you watch presentations, take notes on the material and the speaker

Unless you're still in high school, it doesn't matter if the people sitting next to you think you're some kind of teacher's pet because you take notes. Always take pen and paper along. As you listen and watch, try to absorb not only the subject matter, but also what you do and do not like about the presenter. If you find the visual aids particularly helpful, jot down why (e.g., "slides short, two points per slide easy to read"). If the audience responds favorably to the speaker, try to make a note of that ("quote from Einstein got attention"). Likewise, note a speaker's habits that seemed to be unpleasant or ineffective ("never looked up from script" or "spoke in monotone").

Taking notes doesn't need to be a painful or gleefully critical exercise. Simply give the mechanics of the presentation some thought, and make some notes on what you liked and didn't like. Next time you're feeling stress at the prospect of giving your own speech, you can simply look back and say, "Hey, I liked it when so-and-so looked up at the audience while she talked. I can do that," or "I found it very interesting when my supervisor started his speech with a quote, and that's how I'm going to start mine."

An added benefit of this practice is to observe how other speakers interact with and field questions from their audiences. In my experience as a teaching librarian, I often noticed that my colleagues were most unsettled by the possibility of having to interact with their classes, especially how to respond to the session's more vocal (sometimes belligerent) students. Many different methods of dealing with such situations exist, and the best way to find those is to be there when someone else demonstrates them. I myself never would have thought that simply pointing to people and pleasantly requesting an answer to my question (although it's always important to immediately pick someone else if your first choice seems ill at ease) would have worked until I saw it done. In every class I taught thereafter, I was able to use that technique to encourage students to take part in any discussion.

Listening analytically to speeches and presentations with the hope of improving your own skills is something that, just like speaking, gets easier with practice. Watch the speaker carefully from start to finish and structure your notes in the same way:

✓ How did the speaker enter the room and introduce himself?

✓ How did she begin, and did she manage to engage your interest?

✓ Were you, as the listener, offered any accompanying materials, and did the speaker begin by outlining his goals and expectations?

✓ What was the speaker wearing, and how did she look while talking?

✓ When he concluded, did he thank the audience or offer any opportunities for them to provide feedback?

That is not, of course, an exhaustive list, but just a few of the most easily observed characteristics of speeches and presentations. Writers of presentation design textbooks also encourage listeners to note how and why electronic presentations are used; "in other words, use a separate channel in your mind to monitor how the presentation looks and how the presenter behaves during the presentation" (Joss 1999, 2). Areas of electronic delivery to consider include how the screens are designed, how color has been used, how the text looks, and what graphics were used.

Readers and writers will tell you that there's something magical and powerful about the action of putting words down on paper. In his book on public speaking techniques for scientists and engineers, Peter Kenny noted that observation provides the opportunity for analysis, and that "you can learn much about the skill of public speaking by observing the performance of others and of yourself" (Kenny 1982, 101). So, take a notebook and pen along to your meetings, roundtable discussions, and presentations, and make that power work for you well before you take the podium.

You can listen to others, but you have to know yourself

After you've seen a variety of presentations, and taken some notes on techniques and speaking mannerisms that you do and do not like, you are ready to apply what you've learned to your own style of presentation. At this point, however, I would caution you to take some words of advice from Hamlet himself: "This above all: to thine own self be true." Just because a technique worked for another speaker and you noticed it, does not mean that it will work for you. The key is to observe what works for other speakers (and why) and how you can adapt those same principles to your

own talks. You may have been persuaded by a speaker who used strong language and disconcerting statistics, but if you are not comfortable appealing to the emotions of others, it is likely that your discomfort will show when you are trying to present unpleasant or startling facts in your own speech. Know yourself, and watch other speakers to gather ideas on the different ways of getting and keeping an audience's attention.

A supervisor of mine (a very nice supervisor) once quite seriously told me that she was trying to insert more humorous anecdotes into her library instruction presentations. She was sincere in her desire to improve her presentation skills, but she was no stand-up comedian, and every time she tried to make a joke, it fell flat — providing nothing more than a constant source of frustration to her. One day she admitted she was not Conan O'Brien, but that she enjoyed watching him. She adjusted. Rather than attempting a stand-up routine, she showed a cartoon that illustrated her point perfectly, and because she was comfortable doing that, the students responded to her positively.

Knowing yourself and your own work style will not only help with your actual speech, but also in the creation of it. Give some thought to how you fulfill any of your work duties, and use your own style to efficiently prepare your talk. When you know you have to do something, do you usually prefer to do it immediately, rather than wait until right before it's expected to be done? Then start work on your expected presentation immediately, even if you are tempted to put it off because public speaking is not your favorite thing to do. Follow that principle, and the familiarity of your own work and personal style will not only be comforting in its consistency, but will help the format and words you choose be more appropriate for you.

John Hilton, a well-known BBC broadcaster in the 1930s, said it best when he said, "You may even, I think, copy or mimic someone else's style now and again just to see if there's anything in it that fits you. But in the end, you've got to find your own self" (Safire 1992, 526).

Know your audience, and they'll listen to you

So you've seen some speakers, you've noted some techniques, and you've taken into account your working style. Now you're ready to think about those other people in the room with you: that's right, you're not going to be talking to yourself in there. You're going to have an audience, and it really *is* all about their wants and needs.

If you've ever sat through an introductory communications class or read any communication theory, you know that a lot of energy goes into describing models of communication. One of the most famous communication theories, the mathematical theory of communication, was provided by two telecommunications experts: "The information source selects a desired message out of a set of possible messages. The transmitter changes this message into the signal which is actually sent over the communication channel from the transmitter to the receiver" (Shannon and Weaver 1949, 7). That model and others are often accompanied by complicated diagrams that show a "sender" (the speaker) delivering the "message" to their "receiver" (the audience) in a left-to-right, complete-with-directional-arrows kind of

way, with allowances made for any number of distracting factors, known as "noise," that can interfere with the reception of the message. It was a groundbreaking definition, and is a standard in the field, but I think it does a grave disservice to anyone approaching the already-daunting task of public speaking. It gives the impression that the speaker and the receivers are on opposing sides, not only of the room, but of the process.

What many speakers forget is that they and the audience are actually on the same side. No one wants to give a bad presentation, and no one wants to listen to one, so we're all there with a common goal. It can be very heartening to realize that the audience actively *wants* you to succeed; after all, they don't want to go back to their own jobs and lives convinced that they just lost another hour they'll never get back. The best metaphor for this is offered by speech trainers Deb Gottesman and Buzz Mauro: "Your audience is essentially on the stage with you, an integral part of the scene. You're not creating something for them; you're creating something with them" (Gottesman and Mauro 2001, 13).

Many public speaking textbooks will start you off by asking you to pick a topic, and then to distill it to one single sentence, a sort of theme statement. That's a good organizational exercise, but often inapplicable for librarians and other informational professionals who usually have their topics chosen for them. If it falls to you to give patrons a tour of your library, you don't have the option of speaking to them about knitting (except perhaps as you pass by the 746s) which is really your true love. Even the basic outline of your speech may not be too flexible (let's face it, people on a tour are going to expect to learn where the bathrooms and copy machines are), but you must consider how to make the experience as helpful as possible for your specific audience. If you're expecting an elementary-school class, you will want to spend more time in the children's book room and less time describing where the tax forms can be found.

It is often said that part of the great appeal of Frank Sinatra's singing was his penchant for always singing the same song differently in order to keep himself and his listeners interested. Consider what you have to say to whom, and then sing your song their way.

Chapter Summary

Anyone who watched ABC's *Schoolhouse Rock* cartoons in the mid–1970s could tell you that "Knowledge is Power!" As a starting point for improving your speaking skills and learning to view your speaking or presentation duties as opportunities to be welcomed rather than ordeals to be feared, it is imperative for you to watch and learn from others, as well as from yourself. Become a better speaker by first becoming a better listener: Actively listen to others. Observe and learn from what they do. Get to know yourself, and after that, endeavor to get to know your future audience. All of these strategies will endear you not only to the people to whom you'll be speaking, but also to those who speak to you. No matter how secure any of us are, it's always nice to look out at a pleasant face, an audience member who is engaged in what we're saying and giving us positive feedback.

It has been estimated by communication researchers that, in the course of our workdays, each of us spends seventy to eighty percent of our waking hours in verbal communication activities, and "of this, nearly half, or forty-five percent or more is spent listening. People speak only thirty percent of the time; read sixteen percent of the time, and write only about nine percent of the time" (Smith 1986, 247). Anything you spend almost half of your life doing, you should want to do well, especially when you know that it can provide big dividends when it's your turn to prepare and give your own presentation.

CHAPTER 2

Doing the Prep Work

If you have a question, don't hesitate to ask a librarian.
— Stephen E. Lucas, *The Art of Public Speaking*

If you thought listening to others give presentations was easy, you're going to think this chapter's strategies are an absolute snap. It's true that Jacques Barzun, a prominent education and social scientist, once referred to librarians and journalists as "intellectual middlemen, who confuse the assembling of items found here and there with real research" (Crowley 1996, 116), but I don't agree. I can't speak for journalists, but if there's one thing we know how to do, it's research. I don't think the limb I'm going out on is too long when I say that at work most of us would rather stay in the background, doing research for ourselves or others (often doing more than is even necessary) than do anything else.

If you've followed the suggestions in the first chapter and listened to others, viewed their presentations, and taken some notes on content and style, you've already done a significant amount of research; you've seen that others can speak in public and live, and you might even have learned some techniques for effective organization and speaking. Eventually, of course, you'll have to stop attending every presentation you can, because you'll have

to start the preparatory research for your own speaking engagement. That should be good news; as a librarian or information professional, performing research should be second nature to you. Using that research effectively while preparing and speaking may well be another matter, but for now, revel in the fact that you get to engage hard-core in what probably drew you to the library in the first place.

Doing the Research: Listing What You Know, Looking Up What You Don't

The first misstep to avoid is assuming that you probably already know more about your subject matter than you need to, or than does your audience. It's an easy enough mistake to make; after all, they're taking the time to listen to your presentation, aren't they? People who knew everything about your subject matter wouldn't bother, right? Wrong. If anything, the chances are good that if they're interested enough to attend your presentation, they're interested enough to have done some of their own learning

13

in the area. Even if their attendance at your particular event is not voluntary, you could still be surprised at the depth of your audience members' knowledge (and, conversely, the shallowness of your own).

I learned this the hard way during an introductory public speaking class in my first year of college. Our second speech assignment was to give an informative speech on the subject of our choice. After a typical late night of watching cartoons on cable, I decided I would speak about my first true love: Bugs Bunny. I owned Looney Toons t-shirts, I'd been watching Bugs Bunny cartoons since childhood, I knew that Mel Blanc hated carrots and would immediately spit them out after chewing them up for the soundtrack. I figured I could easily make up three minutes' worth of information to present to my class, and congratulated myself on having avoided the extra work of a trip to the library. The morning of the day I was to give my speech, I stopped by my professor's office to ask her a question … and saw, on the bookcase behind her, an entire shelf of books on animation, Warner Bros. cartoons, and Bugs Bunny. I remember sprinting from her office to the stacks in the hopes that I could hastily assemble some facts on note cards that would supplement what I had thought to be my superlative knowledge.

You may already know your topic, and because of your information-seeking profession, you certainly know how to research. Now, like any beginning speech student, you must fully utilize both of those skills to your fullest potential. The steps listed in this chapter are designed to make you use your subject knowledge to perform the best research possible, so when the time comes to organize your information (which I'll discuss in the next chapter), you'll be ready.

List what you feel will be the main points of your presentation

Before you do research, or before you begin to organize the order of your speech, take just a moment to sit down and make a quick list of the points you would like to or are obliged to make. Leave some space between the points; you'll see why later. For now you shouldn't be concerned with the why or how of your presentation, but should be asking yourself, "What five main ideas do I want my audience to take away from this presentation?" Depending on the situation and time constraints, be careful to formulate achievable goals, remembering that you will not always have the full attention of the class. Research on the attention span of students in lectures indicates that, following an initial three to five minute "settling down" period at the beginning of the class, "the next lapse of attention usually occurred some ten to eighteen minutes later, and as the lecture proceeded the attention span became shorter and often fell to three or four minutes towards the end of a standard lecture" (Johnstone and Percival 1976, 49–50).

For example, let's say that you have been asked to give a one-hour workshop on the use of a new e-books service that your public library is offering. Many people have been asking questions about how to access and use the new service, and have indicated some frustration with the product's less-than-friendly user interface. You sit down and make a list of what you believe to be the main characteristics of the new e-book product:

1. Anyone with a library card can access e-books.

2. Advantages of e-books include availability, and keyword searchability.

3. E-books can be read in a variety of ways.

4. The service is free to patrons, and is paid for by the library.

5. There is a great variety of titles available.

As I stated earlier, don't concern yourself with organization or tiny factual details for the moment. For now, you should simply be considering what knowledge, in an ideal world, you'd like your audience to take with them from your presentation. Trying to be idealistic and organized in one small step will only overwhelm you and contribute to your speaking anxieties. The points listed in the example just given are short for a reason; you can only cover so much ground in any workshop, and even five main points will be more than enough work to research and present adequately. It will also be more than enough for your audience to remember; research shows that people forget twenty-five percent of what they hear within twenty-four hours, fifty percent within forty-eight hours, and eighty percent in four days (Leeds 1991, 55).

Fill in what you know about your main points

Many times you will already have a decent store of knowledge regarding your chosen or assigned topic, and now is the time to put that knowledge to work. Again, using the example already started, consult your list and write down supporting information (which you al-ready know) for your main points. At the end of this step, the list might look something like this:

1. Anyone with a library card can access e-books.

   a. To apply for a library card, you must show a picture ID and proof of current address.

   b. To access e-books, you will have to provide your entire nine-digit ID number.

2. Advantages of e-books include availability and keyword searchability.

   a. If you have Internet access at home, you can access e-book titles twenty-four hours a day, seven days a week.

   b. There is no limit to the number of patrons who can access one book at the same time.

   c. You can search the full text of e-books by any keywords.

3. E-books can be read in a variety of ways.

   a. You can read e-books online or download them to print out sections of the text to read or study.

   b. E-books can be used in the library for quick research of reference books not owned by the library.

4. The service is free to patrons, and is paid for by the library.

   a. Your public library consortium (a governing group that is part of the county's public library system) pays a flat fee for access to a certain set of titles.

5. There is a great variety of titles available.

   a. The library owns e-book titles that

it does not own in print, for greater access to more books.

b. The e-book service includes fiction and nonfiction titles, as well as Cliffs Notes and reference books.

So that, at quick glance, is the basic outline of what you want to say and what you already know. Not bad. With a little luck and some question-and-answer time, that's enough information to provide a helpful introduction to your electronic books service. Once you get beyond your nervousness, and as you give more presentations, you'll be continually surprised to discover how fast time goes, and how even a little bit of information can go a very long way. Now, however, with your ideas firmly in place, you can finally and efficiently start your supplementary formal research and explore the intricacies of the product, as well as flesh out the bare bones of your presentation.

Perform supplementary research

Turning to your colleagues, books, the Internet, and other reference sources, you now need to delve as deeply as possible into your subject matter. This is a strategy I'm not going to belabor; authors of other public speaking books often suggest that a speaker "search out the reference librarian and make friends with someone who knows about research" (McManus 1998, 50), so, Barzun excluded, the consensus is that you know how to find and use information.

Assume that you spend your research time speaking with a co-worker, reading the e-books product homepage, and reading a journal article about the use of electronic book products. Librarian Laura Sullivan advises gathering

more content than you ever plan to use, and then sorting through it to find the best and most useful material: "This step allows you the luxury of editing and, if need be, recognizing any information gaps that need to be filled" (Sullivan 1994, 710).

One cautionary note: as a busy student or professional, I'm sure you've got more than enough to do. As tempting as it may be to indulge in endless research, don't get bogged down to the point of neglecting other necessary preparations. It has been suggested by numerous speaking experts that approximately sixty percent of your speech preparation time should be devoted to researching and writing it — and the rest of your time to developing and practicing it (McManus 1998, 4).

Find one little-known or interesting piece of information about your topic

Although research can be fun and engaging, you're going to have to jerk yourself back to reality and start preparing yourself for the actual presentation aspect of your speech. One nice way to round off your research and propel yourself into the next step is to glean one nugget of information about your subject that you find interesting, and which you suspect not many other people besides you might know. For example, in the course of researching how people use e-books, you may have learned that the best e-book reader screen currently available has a resolution of 100 dots per inch, compared to the average book's 1200 dots per inch resolution (giving books 144 times the resolution and making them easier to read) (Hage and Sottong 2000, 61). Not only will knowing this piece of trivia enhance your overall confidence regarding your knowledge of the subject matter, you may well end up using it later as an introductory hook, a transitional fun fact, or a closing remark. Incidentally, however, that particular piece of information may not help you make a compelling case for the use of e-books. Still, it's a good thing to know and understand (the comfort level of reading from a computer screen is likely to be raised during a workshop discussion or question-and-answer session).

Revisit your list and complete it with the inclusion of information researched

Hopefully you're not too sick of your list yet, because it's now time to return to it. It's not enough to have done your research, you need to drop what you've learned into the spaces where it's going to do the most good. Continuing the e-books example, your final list could look something like this:

1. Anyone with a library card can access e-books.

   a. To apply for a library card, you must show a picture ID and proof of current address.

   b. To access e-books, you will have to provide access to your entire nine-digit ID number.

      i. In addition to your library card ID number, you must register online to use the product, and select a user name and password (which you will have to remember to be able to log in in the future).

      ii. When registering, you will be asked to provide an e-mail address.

2. Advantages of e-books include availability and keyword searchability.

   a. If you have Internet access at home, you can access e-book titles twenty-four hours a day, seven days a week.

      i. The best time of day to view or download e-book titles is in the very early morning or evening; library usage statistics prove that the product is most often accessed during the afternoon hours, and that increased traffic can negatively impact the system's speed.

   b. There is no limit to the number of patrons who can access one book at the same time.

      i. More than one patron may view the same book at the same time, but only thirty-six simultaneous users may be logged into the system.

   c. You can search the full text of e-books by any keywords.

      i. This makes e-books, especially classic literature titles, a great option when doing book reports or papers on such aspects of the book as word usage, metaphor, and imagery.

      ii. Searching by keyword can also be very useful when using e-book software and computer manual titles; you can automatically link to related information and tips within the text.

3. E-books can be read in a variety of ways.

a. You can read e-books online or download them to print out sections of the text to read or study.

    i. Downloading a 150-page title takes about five minutes.

b. E-books can be used in the library for quick research of reference books not owned by the library.

    i. Approximately 200 titles currently included in the e-books database are reference books the library does not own.

4. The service is free to patrons, and is paid for by the library.

a. Your public library consortium (a governing group that is part of the county's public library system) pays a flat fee for access to a certain set of titles.

    i. The subscription costs $12,000 per year, and is split between the county's libraries. The cost for all libraries to own the titles included in the product would be many times that.

5. There is a great variety of titles available.

a. The library owns e-book titles that it does not own in print, for greater accessibility to more books.

    i. Your branch library owns 40,000 books, and can access 15,000 more titles as e-books.

    ii. Most titles available as e-books that are not available in print are computer and software manuals.

    iii. The next greatest number of available e-books are reference titles the library can't afford in print, such as the *Directory of Software Manufacturers* (which can be useful for those researching various software products, or job-searching).

b. The e-book service includes fiction and nonfiction titles, as well as Cliffs Notes and reference books.

    i. Your branch library does not purchase Cliffs Notes. Unless you order Cliffs Notes titles from other county libraries, and wait for them to arrive, the e-books product is the only place they're available.

    ii. More nonfiction titles are available than fiction, currently. Most fiction titles included are from university presses, and many fiction bestsellers are not available.

While doing research, compile a bibliography

Throughout the research process, be careful to record your sources. There are a variety of ways to do so; invest in a bibliographic management software tool (or download one for free from the Internet; a list of free products can be found by searching the Literacy Information listserv archive at http://bubl. ac.uk/mail/bild/, by the keywords "bibliographic builder"), make photocopies or copies of book title pages or Internet sites that you consult and make your notes directly on them, simply list your sources on a piece of notebook paper, or list your sources and notes on separate note cards. If you do that, you'll find that you've not only prepared your speech, you've inadvertently created a helpful handout, and there are very few situations where a comprehensive bibliography will not prove to be an invaluable resource for you and your audience.

In addition to serving as an audience handout, compiling a bibliography will be especially valuable if you intend to prepare an electronic slide show or computer presentation. When presenting information in the form of lists, charts, illustrations, or other graphic layouts, it is imperative that you list your source material right on the slide or webpage (this both increases the chance that your audience will view you as credible and provides the information necessary for the audience to consult your sources, should they wish to). If you compile your source list at the same time you do your research, you won't have to worry about chasing down page references and source citations the night before your presentation, when you're already running out of time to create your accompanying electronic presentation. Somehow, there's never quite enough time to fully prepare, and the last thing you want to be doing right before your presentation is frantic zero-hour citation searching. Diligently record every single source you use; leaving out even one or two can come back to haunt you.

Chapter Summary

An important part of achieving success as a speaker is to be well-versed in your subject matter, a requirement which often requires a speaker to perform at least some basic preparation and research. Librarians, among professionals, are uniquely qualified (not to mention often physically situated near research tools and resources) to efficiently locate information; we must use that research proficiency when formulating our presentations.

To support your talk's main points and to be ready for any questions or challenges that may be presented by your audience, you must first list your main points, write down what you know about them, perform necessary supplementary research, make notes of interesting trivia and essential facts regarding your subject, and carefully (and completely) record your source material information.

Communications researcher and professor Stephen Lucas advises readers of his public speaking textbook that librarians "can help you find your way, locate sources, even track down a specific piece of information" (Lucas 1998, 130). Only after doing that for yourself can you turn to the next step in the speaking preparation process: organizing the *what* you've got to say into the *how* and *when* of saying it.

CHAPTER 3

Imposing Order (You Know You Want To)

Tell them what you're going to tell them; tell them; then tell them what you've told them.

— Popular public speaking adage

Any library layperson, especially if forced to peruse either the AACR2 or the Library of Congress Subject Headings, might opine that librarians love to organize things (although the less kind might suggest that we have too much time on our hands as well as a maniacal need for order).

Regardless of how you view the recent surge in literature and library-school discussion decrying the problem of our bookish and nerdy image, now is the time to be proud of your classification and detail-oriented heritage. Such traits will be invaluable as you organize your speech, and you should approach the task with all the sincerity and joy with which our predecessors first attempted to cram the whole of human knowledge onto catalog cards.

Walking the Talk: Applying Your Organizational Skills to Your Presentation

So far you have developed and used your listening skills to learn how other speakers organize their talks and approach their audiences, and you should have prepared a short list of main points you'd like to cover in your own (as well as performed the research to corroborate them). Before you can stand up and face your own audience, you have to structure your talk so that it is logical to you, think of ways to introduce and summarize your topic, and create your handouts or visual aids.

Contrary to popular belief, organization requires imagination, because you have to put yourself in your listeners' shoes. If you're a public librarian, you might have to pretend that you'd never read a certain genre or author; if you were a freelancer, you might need to ask yourself why some publisher who doesn't know you would possibly want to hire you based on your introduction at a conference. For this chapter's speech formulation example, imagine yourself to be an academic librarian preparing an introductory workshop on your university's online catalog. You've already settled on a list of main topics that you hope to cover on behalf of your audience, which will consist of first-year students who, you believe, are not familiar with the campus library system. Your list appears as follows (for the sake of brevity, main points only are listed):

1. The catalog is easy to access and use.

2. There are two main types of searches: guided and basic.

3. The most common search performed is for periodical titles.

4. The "results" lists includes the titles and their campus library locations.

5. The catalog also includes live Internet links to websites and e-journals.

For this particular example, the question you have to ask yourself is, "If I were looking at the catalog for the first time, what questions would I have, and in what order?" As information mediators we should be used to dealing with a myriad of questions, and should therefore be better equipped than most to silence our own hypothetical inquiries with references and organization.

I have found that many public speaking textbooks advocate following any number of ordering principles, from the chronological to that of answering the journalistic questions of who, what, where, when, why, and how. Speeches can also be classified by their intended purpose: to inform, to persuade, to demonstrate, to introduce, and so on.

However, we must understand that we are not introductory speech students and that we will not be graded on how well we follow structural principles. What counts here is clarity. Instead of focusing your energy on which ordering scheme to follow, simply work out the order that seems most logical to you. We make our living arranging and accessing information for our users, and that is really all you are doing when you are preparing your speech. Trust your instincts.

Organize your list so that it makes sense to you

To continue our earlier example, face your list while simultaneously using your online catalog as though you had never seen it before. Picture yourself sitting down in front of a library terminal for the first time. Knowing your audience (recent data suggests that eighty percent of first-year college students have experience with computers) helps you decide to keep any introductory advice on how to work the mouse to a minimum, but imagining that you have never searched your library catalog for a book might lead you to wonder, "How do I access the catalog?" and before you know it, you've got your first and most important point. After you open the catalog, what search screen are you in? What do the words "basic" and "guided" mean, anyway? How come there isn't a "search for magazines" button? Once you've actually chosen a particular title, where on campus do you go to get your hands on it?

Those are all very logical and well-ordered queries, exactly as they arrive. Move through the entire catalog, doing searches for whatever you're interested in, or believe your students might find useful, and take notes to slow yourself down and keep a record of the process of research. When you are done, you should find that you have again inadvertently solved your organizational problems by simply thinking about how your audience would approach the subject, rather than artificially forcing the topic into an arbitrary chronological or other framework. If your school library catalog is anything like some of those I have worked with, you might have arrived at the same order as I did for your main points:

✓ The catalog is easy to access, from the library or from home.

✓ The catalog allows you to search for a variety of sources, including books, journals (but not journal articles) and Internet links.

✓ To search for those items, you will most often use either the basic or the guided search options.

✓ The basic search is best when you know an exact title or author, and is most effective for searching by journal title.

✓ The guided search is best for searching by related subjects.

✓ The catalog results screen will tell you where on campus certain resources can be found, and whether or not they are currently available.

Think of a way to introduce your subject matter and engage your audience

Now that you have your main points and a rough idea of the order in which you will present them, it is time to move on to what has always been, un-

questionably, my favorite part of creating a presentation. It is now time to think of your "hook," the way you will grab the attention of your audience. Again, many public speaking textbooks and even informal books of hints and suggestions for would-be speakers often present lists of proven techniques for introductions, including the use of quotations, statistics, a personal story, or perhaps just the reason the audience will benefit from your talk (also known as the "what's in it for me" factor). Using humor is also commonly cited as a successful method of getting people to sit up and take notice; "humor works extremely well as an attention-getting device, and when humor is closely tied to an instructional point, its value is compounded" (Antonelli 2000, 180). Employing an element of surprise is another way to reach out and seize the moment and the attention of your audience. Not surprisingly, communication theorists, such as Emory Griffin, have advanced that approach. Whichever way you choose to start your presentation, you stand a better chance of both you and your topic being remembered if your beginning is completely original or even slightly out of the ordinary; "Should you communicate in a totally unexpected way? If you're certain that the novelty will be a pleasant surprise, the answer is yes" (Griffin 2000, 87).

That said, I cannot adequately express the importance of making sure that you're comfortable with your introduction, both the method and content. If divulging the (albeit strikingly relevant) details of your personal life is not even something you do with your best friend, no amount of textbook examples touting such sharing as a proven and efficacious public speaking "technique" will put you at ease, and if there's one thing an audience can sense and distrust, it's a speaker's personal discomfort. Likewise, if you are not a person who reads or finds inspiration in quotations, do not woodenly read a quote — even the perfect quote — off a note card. You do not have to follow a proscribed technique, nor should you have to buy a speaking book outlining the different types of introductions. Take some time and think about how you normally introduce yourself in social situations. How do you get people's attention at work, or at home? Do you like to joke around when you interact with people, or are you a person who has a good memory for facts and figures, and can relate them at a moment's notice in meetings and other speaking situations? If anything, it is probably best to take traditional speaking "rules" with a grain of salt. For example, many books suggest appealing to people's emotions if you want to be persuasive, and even never opening with a joke if you want to be effective, yet how many times have we been persuaded by humor or convinced by reason?

I very rarely get upset about the current state of higher education, but I did so recently when a friend of mine related that he had been told by his college speech professor "never to use humor, because so few people can pull it off." He had worked a joke into a speech for class, and even though the audience laughed, and responded well (he is naturally quite funny), the professor graded him harshly for not following *his* rules. My point is that although you should be aware enough of your own personality and style to know which techniques may or may not work for you, do not be constrained by traditionally held tenets of "public speaking." If you know a great

joke that is relevant to your subject matter, and you are completely comfortable telling it to a roomful of people, please do so. For every instance you can find in the literature suggesting that you stay away from comedy, you will find another extolling its necessity. Kurt Vonnegut once advised that if you have to give a speech, start with a joke. After beginning a commencement address with a riddle of his own (Why is cream more expensive than milk? Because the cows hate to squat on those little bottles), he went on to explain: "How do jokes work? We are such earnest animals. When I asked you about cream, you could not help yourselves. You really tried to think of a sensible answer" (Vonnegut 1981, 176). Therein he illustrated two principles of good speaking: try to get the audience involved in some way, and make your introductory quotation or fact or joke one that you enjoy personally; Vonnegut referred to the cream joke as the funniest one he knew.

If you aren't lucky enough to have someone else introduce you, you may face one of the biggest hurdles of any speaker: before getting the audience's attention, you must first remove it from whoever or whatever already has it. Whether you're facing a group of students, a roomful of chatty book-group patrons, or a conference audience, there is often a great deal of chatter and other noise present right before you have to stand up and speak your piece. At that moment, it is best not to fight the noise, but simply to "try standing still, even if it is uncomfortable. Being still gives your listeners a focus: you" (Glickstein 1998, 97). It may truly be uncomfortable, but try not to speak before your audience is ready to hear you; it may feel like an eternity, but if you stand in front of the room with an open and receptive smile on your face, the audience's gradual awareness of your presence will compel them to grant you attention. If it's feasible, the exact opposite can also be performed, with some success. Two friends and I once had to give a presentation to a library-school class, and since we were the first presenters, there was quite a bit of talking and pre-class commotion, even though, technically, our class time had already begun. I was scheduled to introduce our subject — religious libraries and their users — and planned to open with a quote made famous by the movie *Pulp Fiction*: Samuel L. Jackson's tirade from the biblical book of Ezekiel ("The path of the righteous man is beset on all sides by the iniquities of the wicked…."). I had chosen the quote to indicate that even cult filmmakers sometimes consulted the Bible, and because I thought it would be fun to say. When the chatter refused to die down, even though my friends and I were in the front of the room, and our professor was trying, subtly, to bring the room to order, I decided to step up without further adieu and belt the quote out. By the time I was finished with the entire thing, not only had a rather shocked classroom silence descended, but I had my classmates' attention, as they were clearly wondering why I was shouting biblical passages at them. Sure, I was called "Preacher" for the rest of the semester, but my co-presenters and I enjoyed putting on our show, so that was a small price to pay.

To revisit a technique introduced in the second chapter, the beginning of your speech is where the little-known or particularly interesting nuggets of information gleaned from your solid research work may occasionally come in handy. Consult your notes and consider whether any of the facts or statistics you have gathered and organized there might be enticing enough to offer during your grand opening. Later in this book you will find an appendix of speech preparation materials, and my suggestion that you maintain a tickler file containing anecdotes, facts, jokes, and other pieces of information seductive enough to keep (in the course of specific topic research as well as your general reading); then you'll have them on hand the next time you're called on to give a talk. Kurt Vonnegut provided me with a joke, so I'll return the favor by passing on my own favorite: Why did the elephant paint his toenails red? So he could hide in the strawberry patch!

Think of a way to summarize and conclude your presentation

Immediately following my favorite aspect of speech preparation, I am faced with my least favorite task: formulating a summary and conclusion. I've never understood why I struggle so with that; perhaps, because I like talking, I don't want to stop, or perhaps I'm so excited and ready to go after coming up with my introductory hook that I want to quit preparing and just give the talk. But I know giving up the podium takes preparation as well. Again, personal styles will differ and you may well discover that forming your conclusion, with its promise of finishing your talk, the most enjoyable part of the whole process. One of the librarians whom I interviewed in the course of writing this book told me that she hates preparing introductions, and is certain she is bad at doing so, but she has no difficulties whatsoever writing and delivering her summations and conclusions.

Let's take a moment to review. By now you have a comprehensive outline, supported by evidence and other source material, as well as what you hope will be an attention-getting introduction. Just as it is important to preview your talk for your audience, to prepare them for the knowledge you wish to impart to them, it is important to review the main points of your speech at its close. Have you ever heard the conventional wisdom that it is best to present, or to interview, in either the first or last position? That is because people tend to remember what they hear in the beginning of any situation, when they're still alert, as well as near the very end of any situation, because that is when their attention is excited by the prospect of being done. So, in many ways, your introduction and your conclusion will be the most-heard and best-remembered parts of your talk, and if you can condense your information into easily remembered points (think verbal bullet points) and present them at both ends of your presentation, you increase your chances of being heard, understood, and remembered by your audience.

Public speaking differs from another important method of communication, writing, in the degree of redundancy that you must include in your spoken presentation. Writers often try to avoid redundancy, in word and in thought, because they know their readers can simply re-read any portions of the text that they don't clearly understand as well as those they particularly enjoyed. The people who will be listening to you do not have that luxury, which is why you have to tell them what you're going to tell them (in the introduction), tell them (in the body), and then tell them what you've told them (in the conclusion). That is why it is not often recommended that you write a speech and read it to your audience word-for-word; if you've written something well, it simply will not include enough redundancy for your audience to fully grasp what you're saying.

Summing up should not present any great difficulty. Simply revisit your outline and repeat the main points that you listed for yourself and your audience. If time permits and you consider it necessary or even helpful, you may present one small piece of corroborating information with your main points. For example: "Last year, sixty percent of first-year students reported they brought computers with them, so if you're one of them, please remember you can search the catalog at home, but we love to see you in the library, and there are always openings on our computers here to search the catalog."

In addition to restating your main points, you may want to finish with a concluding thought or synthesizing idea. The many books on public speaking currently available have less to say on techniques for finishing a talk than for starting one, although many of the same techniques that apply to introductions (quotations, statistics, anecdotes, etc.) can be used effectively with conclusions. One surefire way to end things on a friendly note is to offer further assistance, or to indicate your availability immediately after the presentation and beyond for questions and other comments. Combined with a genuine smile and an expression of gratitude for your audience's attention, an offer of further assistance to your audience cannot miss as a successful ending. After explaining and demonstrating the library catalog to students, any librarian could give a rather dry topic a personal touch: "I'm really glad you came to the library today. My name is Sarah, and you can always find me at the reference desk if you have any questions. Please. If I don't get questions there, I get stuck cataloging technical reports, and that's not going to be good for anyone."

Prepare your visual aids or handouts

Have you ever stopped to wonder why show-and-tell is such a kindergarten standard? Because we learn not only by listening, but by looking, and even touching, as well. There are very few topics or types of presentations that do not lend themselves to the use of visual aids in some way. Even if you don't plan on using presentation software or a live Internet exhibit, you may want to prepare something for your audience to look at. No matter how engaging you are, it's never a bad idea to provide options other than the window for those times when the members of your audience need the occasional change of scenery.

A short appendix outlining techniques for effectively using presentation software and other tools can be found at the end of this book. Remember, however, that long before presentation software, there were other quite functional aids. What about the bibliography of source material you created when you were doing your research? Clean it up, copy it onto colorful paper, and title it "Suggested Resources for Further Reading." Likewise, in the course of your preparation, you created a step-by-step outline of the material you wanted to cover, as well as an introduction and a summary. That same outline can be a

synopsis. If your topic is sufficiently technical, or you plan to move rather quickly, and you think your audience might benefit from a formal treatment of your subject, type it up for use as a handout; doing so serves the added benefit of giving your audience something handy to write on should they want to take any notes. Sales presentation specialist Terri L. Sjodin points out the effectiveness of this resource: "Your single outline handout on a lone sheet of paper will become the most significant presentation piece in your publications package. Why? Because this is the handout your listeners now own. They own it because they put their notes on it. And we always hold on to the one thing for which we feel ownership" (Sjodin 2001, 44). You might even leave space for notes wherever it seems appropriate. Other types of visual aids and handouts you can create include:

✓ Keyboard shortcut or software command "cheat sheets" (for example: "Ctl+N: New Document").

✓ Bookmarks with library maps, hours, contact information, or other library tips.

✓ Screen shots of various programs or Internet resources.

✓ Any kind of chart, graph, or other visual representation of your information.

Is there a certain cartoon, picture, or quotation that you think perfectly illustrates your point? Include it on the bottom of your handout (giving copyright credit where necessary, of course) for a little added zing.

In addition to these types of visuals, which you can easily prepare as you proceed through your preparations, your subject matter will itself suggest different tools and props. If you're giving a book talk, copies of the book or books you're discussing are required, but why not some other books by the author(s), or videotape adaptations of the works discussed, or copies of recent reviews or studies of the featured author? If you are demonstrating dedicated indexing software at an American Society of Indexers conference, consider distributing copies of short samples of indexes created using the software, or copied screen captures of the software interface. An added benefit of such resource creation is the positive effect it can have on your presentation itself; a 1994 study of 119 undergraduate college students found that "The total quantity of preparation time, time spent cognitively processing information related to the speech as well as time spent in silent and oral rehearsal, correlated positively with the quality of thought content and the quality of the speech as a whole" (Menzel and Carrell 1994, 23). One of Menzel and Carrell's suggestions for an activity to cognitively process information related to the speech? You guessed it: spending time creating visual aids.

Chapter Summary

In the midst of your frenzy of research and organization, did you even notice that you were preparing a speech? When facing a speaking engagement, the best offense truly is a good defense; speech anxiety is often caused by a nagging sense of being unprepared, which can be further exacerbated when speakers who truly fear public speaking either delay or avoid thinking about it by refusing to prepare properly. Keep yourself busy organizing your main points, planning a unique introduction, writing a succinct conclusion (including a review of your main points), and producing useful and attractive visual aids and handouts. You'll find you don't have the time (or any need) to fear your turn to stand up and speak, much less worry about whether or not your audience will find you either nerdy or bookish.

CHAPTER 4

The Calm Before the Storm

For most of us, giving a speech is an important and novel event. It's natural and appropriate to feel some anxiety. A speaker's aim should be to keep this natural nervousness from cycling out of control: not to get rid of the butterflies but to make them fly in formation.
— Michael T. Motley, "Taking the Terror Out of Talk"

There's a lot of literature out there that says people should view public speaking less as a "performance" and more as a "conversation," or "pure communication." That is comforting until you look at the shelves of books on public speaking and learn there's an equally large amount of literature urging you to use acting and oratorical skills to improve your performance. What really is the best way to prepare for giving your rapidly approaching speech?

Practice Makes Perfect, but Is Perfection Overrated?

My suggestion: don't give the *process* of speaking too much thought. Obsessing about the tiniest details of your voice tonality, modulation, and your gestures will only make you more anxious than any self-respecting introverted librarian should ever have to be. Focus on your topic. Remember what it is about your subject that excites you,

and try to recapture the enthusiasm you had for it the first time you learned about it, or talked it over with a colleague or a friend. If nothing about your subject excites you particularly (and it will happen, especially if you ever have to report on a project that isn't your own) spend your time finding ways to make it interesting for your audience. Recognize that the superficial details are just that — superficial. Moreover, many of them can be resolved long before you ever have to face your audience.

Have you ever heard the inspirational directive to change what you can, and have the courage to accept what you can't? Increase your chances of speaking confidently by practicing with your visual aids, inspecting your presentation space, rehearsing your speech from start to finish, and enacting personal confidence boosters, and then have the courage to accept that you may still feel some nervousness in spite of all your hard work. Meanwhile, take comfort in the fact that most people can't recognize a speaker's anxiety even when they are trained to do so: "Researchers have found that most people report noticing little or no anxiety in a speaker. Even when individuals are trained to detect anxiety cues and instructed to look for them, there is little correlation between their evaluations and how anxious the speakers actually felt" (Motley 1988, 48).

Learn how to use your visual aids and other performance props

A large part of determining what visual aids and tools you can use effectively is experimenting and practicing with a lot of them. The important thing to remember is that you should never disregard your own style in favor of someone else's suggestion or directive. Librarians do tend to work in an environment that values consensus-building, but when the time comes, you are the one who will be standing in front of the room, alone with whatever visual aids or props you've prepared or chosen to use.

When I was an academic librarian, my library procured a small laser pointer, assuming that all bibliographic instruction librarians would use it during their classes. I don't think laser pointers are a bad tool, and when the lights are down and you're trying to draw the students' attention to one tiny aspect of a crowded search screen, I'll be the first to admit that they can be quite handy. However, whenever I used it, I never failed to feel slightly as if I should be approaching Darth Vader for a light-saber duel. It didn't help that (although my nervousness would lessen over the course of a presentation) my hands were often shaky enough to make the small red pinpoint of light jump frenetically around the screen. After several very unsteady classes using a tool I clearly wasn't comfortable with, I relinquished the pointer to my colleagues and reverted to my former method of pointing at the screen with my index finger (with much improved results). It may not have been as high-tech, but it worked for me.

After you're done experimenting to find the tools that work best for you, you have to devote some time to perfecting your use of them. If you intend to use PowerPoint slides, make sure they're finished long before you'll need them for the presentation, so you can practice speaking along with them. Learn how long it takes for them to load, and spend some time refining them until they're worded exactly the way you want them. Ask a colleague to view a sampling of them to ensure they are easy to read and aesthetically pleasing. The need for preparation extends to nonmechanical tools as well. If you're using a flip book, does it have enough paper and do you have markers that work? If you will present in a setting with a chalkboard that you intend to use, are chalk and erasers are available? Can you comfortably reach most of the board's writing space?

And now (as opposed to those frantic moments before you stand up to talk) is the time to consider when you will distribute handouts or other information to your audience, as well as the form of distribution. Many textbooks and articles advise not handing anything out before (or during) your presentation, because they will distract the audience from you. I find this belittling. It assumes that even before you start, your audience is just looking for ways not to pay attention to you. Besides, if you are providing an outline of your talk that your audience may wish to take notes on, you can't very well distribute it after you've finished.

My two suggestions for timing and method of distribution are these: by all means, hand out everything you've got before the talk, or meeting, or class, and do so by standing at the door or a nearby table and offering the handouts in organized and paper-clipped packets. The rationale behind these suggestions is simple; when you're done talking, you'll want to be just that, done. You will not be in the mood to explain your packets or recapture the attention of your audience, so why not just get it taken care of promptly? Besides, it will boost your confidence immeasurably to project (as you will with such a strategy) the image of a friendly and well-organized librarian.

My first experience with the vast array of handouts that librarians can't help but provide came during a bibliographic instruction practicum I participated in while attending library school. As practicum students, we were expected to assist campus librarians with a number of library instruction sessions for first-year students. For the most part these librarians were skilled and effective, but they never failed to distribute their handouts by setting them out in piles on tables for the students themselves to pick up and assemble, or by handing us various piles and asking students to pass them down the rows. The only thing such a method accomplished on a steady basis was this outburst, minutes into the class: "What handout? I don't have that one," or "We were supposed to pick up handouts?" followed by painful sessions of students trooping back up to the front or shuffling repeatedly through their stacks of paper.

So: put your papers in the order the audience will need them, hand each attendee a packet before he or she sits down, and devote a short minute somewhere early on in your talk to walk participants through the packet and explain the inclusion of each paper. Your coworkers may think you're obsessive, and you may have to raid your organization's supply closet for extra paper clips, but this is one of my favorite speaking tricks. It can be used in meetings, interviews, classes, book talks, conventions, or anywhere else you have something to give to your audience.

And remember, just because you've taken your handouts seriously and prepared them carefully doesn't mean that you can't have a little fun with them as props. I used to share the joy in those first-year classes by telling the students how the individual colors of our instructional packets were carefully deliberated in departmental meetings. They always looked at me like they couldn't quite decide if that was funny or sad, and I got to have a laugh at my own frustration with the micro-planning in our library. More importantly, it drew attention to those colored packets, which was just as it should be, and relaxed the students and their presenter.

Inspect your presentation space

Where you give your presentation can vary widely, depending on the type of speech you're giving, where you normally work, and who your audience will be. If you are a teaching librarian, you may often be asked to present in a college classroom; if you're a public librarian, you may be asked to visit a nursing home to talk about homebound book delivery; every type of librarianship will carry with it its own collection of typical settings. If at all possible, try to visit the room or place in which you will be speaking. The timing makes little difference; you may inspect it early on in your preparations, or you can wait until right before you present (although the latter will leave you with less time to address any possible problems or other issues).

Inspecting your speaking environment is just smart planning. Knowing the acoustics and surroundings of your space will help you adjust your volume and stance appropriately. Depending on the type of presentation you're giving, it will also dictate your time of arrival; for example, if you're moderating a library focus group and want to encourage discussion, you may need to arrive earlier to arrange the room's chairs in a circular pattern (not something you want to be doing when your audience arrives).

When more technical considerations are involved, this step is absolutely required. You will need to know how to work any Internet or projection system that's available for your use, and practicing with it beforehand will not only soothe your nerves but give you the proficiency you'll need to present a seamless demonstration to your audience. You don't have to take a long time doing these things but you do have to be observant. Ask yourself questions and don't leave until you have the answers: Are there blinds you'll have to draw, and can you reach them? Do you know where the light switches are? How do you lower the projection screen, and will it cover up the chalkboard you've just written the necessary URL on? Are there enough chairs for the number of attendees you're expecting? Will your voice carry comfortably to the back of the room, and if not, is a microphone or any other amplification system available?

The bad part of all this is that the responsibility for these technical and environmental concerns will rest squarely on your shoulders, and you may have to suppress your nervousness enough to rationally assess and prepare your surroundings. However, the good part is that this also means you will be in control of your setting (meaning, for example, that if you don't like standing behind lecterns, you can simply remove them) and it will be one less outside concern about which you will have to worry when it's time to give your presentation.

Practice your speech

Now we have come to a subject to which many other speaking manuals devote entire chapters: practice makes perfect, they say, and the more you talk, the more practice you'll get and the better you'll be. I am not about to deny the truth in these maxims, but I would advise that you not focus on this step at the expense of all others. For one thing, everything you've been doing up to this point counts as practice, and effective practice at that. You've already been through your presentation a few times while organizing and researching it, and in preparing and experimenting with your visual aids and environment, you've even practiced the outside factors. For another, excessive preparation can lead to inadvertent memorization of your talk, which can lead to your delivering it without enthusiasm or spontaneity; this has been a recognized problem since the very first century, when Roman scholar and orator Quintilian stated, "He who speaks as though he were reciting forgets the whole charm of what he has written" (McManus 1998, 74).

Many of my colleagues throughout

the years have been big believers in practice, and spent a lot of time in empty rooms nervously reading their prepared words directly from a script. Although this may work for some, those who need the solitude to focus perhaps, such an experience (for me, anyway) was usually more nerve-wracking than the real thing. One of the very best parts of talking to people is just that, the people. When I talk to an empty room I feel none of the nervous excitement but all of the sick dread of standing before an audience. If you find that to be your experience too, consider any nontraditional methods of practicing, or make up your own. I have two favorite practice methods: I either go home and crank the stereo while I pace around my room and work out the words and order of my speech, or I take a walk and run through my speech in my head.

You may also want to practice giving the speech to a friend or colleague; after all, "a practice audience adds an important dimension to preparation and guides the speaker through difficulties that he or she might not notice or correct in a solo rehearsal; moreover, the speaker practicing with an audience can more fully develop the perspective-taking and audience-analysis skills necessary for delivering the speech" (Menzel and Carrell 1994, 23–24). Research on just how much or how little your practice audience should critique you varies widely, from recommending that you receive all criticism to recommending that your practice audience say only positive things, but common sense dictates a mixture of those approaches.

Just as publishers suggest that authors not index their own works, because they are too close to the subject matter, an impartial and honest listener can also help you clarify any parts of your talk that may be potentially confusing or complicated for your real audience, as well as providing feedback regarding performance details such as your rate of eye contact and your voice projection. Encourage your listener(s) to take notes and to ask you questions about your subject; doing so will prepare you for an actual question-and-answer session (another advantage you can't get from talking to an empty room) and may remind you of other facts or information that you may have inadvertently left out of your talk.

If there are time and location restraints, you don't always have to practice at the place where you will give your presentation. Although you will not be able to lug a computer projection system to a coffee shop or lunch, you should certainly be able to take yourself and your note cards; next time you have lunch with a friend, ask that person if he or she would mind listening to a quick outline or the introduction of your upcoming presentation and give you some suggestions. That will also help you realize that your upcoming talk shouldn't be so scary. If you can talk about your subject with a friend over lunch without shaking or throwing up, you've got at least one practice round in, and you should be able to face your audience with greater confidence.

Most importantly, practice should help you get over the notion that you have to use the exact same words every time you give your presentation. What makes me nervous about following a prepared script is precisely this: the notion that I will be a complete failure unless I memorize the most perfectly chosen words. Think about how you converse with your family, your friends, and your co-workers. Do you typically script out every interpersonal communication? Of course not. And do you usually experience stage fright in everyday conversations? Of course not. Think about the link there, and then ask yourself why you would willingly impose upon yourself the stress of memorization before a presentation. When you practice, whether to an empty room or in front of a friend, experiment with using different words, phrases, and gestures. It can be a great exercise in reassurance to realize that sometimes what you have to say really is more important than how you say it.

Enact personal confidence boosters

After you've developed and worked with your visual aids, inspected your presentation space, and practiced your speech, not much stands between you and a successfully completed presentation but its actual delivery. This moment should be the calm before the storm, but it is at just this time that anxiety normally takes hold. Everyone, no matter how polished or professional, experiences at least a small case of the jitters, and you shouldn't expect to be any different. In fact, if you weren't nervous, it might indicate that you didn't care how you were perceived by your audience, and that's the worst thing you can do to yourself and your listeners. In her autobiography, *One More Time*, Carol Burnett admits to having performed once without feeling nervous, and because of her overconfidence, her act tanked. The next time she went on stage she did so nervously, and things went much better (Burnett 1986, 318).

The good news is that studies prove that your nervousness will abate almost immediately after you begin to speak. Speakers' heart rates before starting to talk (the anticipatory stage) often range from about 95 beats per minute to somewhere in the 140s, compared to normal resting heart rates in the 70s. After they begin, their heart rates can jump to 110 to 190 beats per minute, but that surge begins to subside within 30 seconds, quickly returning to the original anticipation rate of 95 to 140 beats per minute, or even lower! (Motley 1988, 48). So accept the fact that you most likely will be nervous before and at the very moment you begin your talk, but remember that you can use your awareness of that fact to calm down and tell yourself, "I'm feeling better already."

When I speak before a group, I often speak from a brief outline or a few note cards. Those are things that only I see, and I keep them close to me at all times, because I've earlier enacted one of my personal favorite confidence boosters: I write my notes (or at least the introduction) in crayon. I vary the colors and keep my sentences short and easy to read, and invariably, when I stand up, take a breath, and look at my notes, it relaxes me to see the sheer ridiculousness of my first sentence written in crayon. How badly can any speech go, I figure, when it started life as an outline or story written in crayon on a note card?

It is also very important that you consider more outward appearances before your presentation. You will not only want to dress appropriately for your topic and your audience, but you will want to dress comfortably. Librarians as a group are not typically known for their cutting-edge style, and dressing appropriately does not mean you have to conform to any other profession's standard of formality. For the most part, you will not have to go out and buy a power suit (with the exception of special librarians, who often do have a more formal business dress code), but you will want to wear something that makes you look good, and more importantly, feel good. If you're not sure what the dress code will be, follow interview logic and dress one step more formally than you think may be required. No one will fault you for that, and the overall impression you should want to give is that this speech of yours is going to be, in some way, a special occasion.

One of the most important things you can do to increase your comfort level during your presentation is to smile, early and often and sincerely. Also, don't be afraid to interact with your audience, and don't hesitate to locate particularly friendly faces on which to focus. For every lethargic listener you have (and they'll be there), you'll find another person in your audience who will listen to you alertly and smile back at you when you make eye contact. Always remember, as I mentioned in the first chapter, that the majority of your audience wants you to do well and is eager to hear what you have to say, so don't be afraid to find your encouraging listeners and speak to them directly. The entire audience will benefit from that, because the more you interact directly with individual members of any group, the less nervous you'll be and the more animated you'll become, which will make it easier for everyone present to pay attention.

Of course, some people will find that a feeling of being prepared is all they need to be able to comfortably and confidently face an audience, as well they should. If you're not one of those lucky people, you will simply have to find your own tricks to take your mind off your nerves, and there's no limit to the form those tricks can take. Write an encouraging and short note to yourself at the midpoint of your speech's notes; take a friend along to the presentation so you're guaranteed at least one friendly face; get a good drink of water and take a deep breath before you begin to speak; the possibilities are endless, and as original and personal as you.

Chapter Summary

Many speakers fall prey to "speech anxiety," the physical symptoms of which include sweaty palms, dry mouth, shaky hands, weak knees, and shortness of breath. Although no amount of preparation or presentation frequency will completely alleviate those and other nervous symptoms (nor would you want it to), you can take action before your speech to increase your confidence and give a successful one. Get comfortable with your visual aids, presentation software, or handouts; practice your speech either alone or in front of others; take the time to carefully investigate the physical space in which you'll be talking, and experiment till you find the confidence boosters that work for you.

Before you turn to the next chapter and its performance suggestions, you may also want to relinquish the idea that your words will be perfect, no matter how much time you spend preparing them. Even one of America's most prominent speech coaches, Lilyan Wilder, recognized that perfection shouldn't be your only goal: "Obsessive devotion to flawlessness, however, can become a genuine obstacle to fearless speaking" (Wilder 1999, 12).

CHAPTER 5

Overture, Curtain, Lights!

Still, the whole business of rhetoric being concerned with appearances, we must pay attention to the subject of delivery, unworthy though it is, because we cannot do without it.

— Aristotle, *Rhetoric*

Not many how-to books get read two millennia after they've been written. It should be comforting to know that not only have people been fearing public speaking since 350 B.C.E., they've also been trying to learn the basic principles and techniques of good oratory, actual speech delivery, which is the subject we turn to now.

On with the Show, This Is It!

Your speech has been researched, organized, and practiced, and now it's show time. That means it's time to trust that the presentation itself is ready, and turn instead to the consideration of the purely aesthetic details of presentation, including voice, stance, word choice, body language, and any number of other performance issues. The most effective methods to improve your speaking skills are to find a voice and a stance that are comfortable for you, choose your words honestly and use them sparingly, observe your audience so that you can adjust your tone and pace to their needs, and to always mentally review your performance when it's over.

Find a voice and stance that are comfortable for you

Celebrities are paid exorbitant amounts of money to do commercial voice-overs, not only because they're celebrities, but because their voices are often well-developed and recognizable because they're distinctive. The good news is that you do not need to become the next James Earl Jones (who, interestingly enough, overcame a stuttering problem on his road to becoming the voice of Darth Vader and Verizon Wireless), but the bad news is that you have to spend some time developing your voice so you can use it effectively when speaking. How important is your voice? Pretty important, if you believe the researchers at UCLA who found that "only seven percent of our credibility with listeners comes from the actual words we speak while thirty-eight percent comes from our vocal qualities" (Dale 1999, 23). You may not think that's fair, but that's the way it is.

Again, a little observation at this point can go a long way. If you're really serious about developing your voice and you have ten dollars to invest, buy a tiny handheld tape recorder. Not only should it give you a cool covert feeling (and how often do librarians get that?), it will help you critique your own voice. Using the tape recorder, or even a stereo or your telephone answering machine at home, tape yourself having a conversation with a friend or simply reading a passage aloud from a book or magazine. The subject matter in this case doesn't matter, but the exercise is most helpful if you can observe the difference between your conversational tone and your presentational tone, so take the time to record examples of both. In which performance do you enunciate more clearly? Which sounds more natural? Which would be better suited to carry to the back of a crowded meeting room? And do spare yourself the agony of obsessing about not liking your own voice. No one does, up to and including George Costanza on *Seinfeld*. I can never believe how high and somewhat thin my voice sounds on tape; that doesn't, however, mean I have a terrible voice. It just means that I'm a soprano, and I have to be aware that the faster I talk and the more excited I get, the higher and thinner my voice gets. The important thing is that I'm aware of it, and after making a few short recordings, you'll know more about your voice qualities, too.

Have you ever stopped to wonder how your vocal cords actually work? They do so in a multitude of ways, really: "The musculature of the larynx is so complicated that you can control the tension in the vocal cords, their length (by changing the angles that the different pieces of cartilage make with each other), their shape, and whether they're in contact over their entire length or parted slightly, like a shirt forced open at the bottom by a beer belly" (Ingram 1992, 32). For more information on how the vocal cords actually produce sound, I would suggest reading books like Jay Ingram's *Talk Talk Talk* or any other book that is devoted to voice training and production (and there are a lot of them out there; three of my favorites are *Voice Power: Using Your Voice to Captivate, Persuade, and Command Attention*; *You Look Great, but How Do You Sound?*; and *The Power of Speech*—their citation information can be found in the bibliography).

If you are truly not happy with the natural volume of your voice, don't fret. Tools do exist to make sure everyone hears you. In some very large lecture or convention halls, some type of microphone may always be necessary (and is probably readily available) just so you don't have to strain yourself or your voice to be heard. For the most part, however, and for most library presentations, your audience should be small enough that your natural volume should be sufficient. Nevertheless, it is always useful to be able to increase the volume and the power of your voice; to do so, you must first learn how to breathe effectively.

Jay Ingram's work on the mechanics of speaking also includes the dynamics of breathing when speaking: "Normally we breathe in and out fifteen times a minute. Inhaling for talking is much faster than normal inhalation. But exhalation is much slower so that more words can be spoken as the air flows out. The result is that when you talk you spend much more of your time breathing out than breathing in: about ninety-five percent vs. five percent" (Ingram 1992, 29–30). To compensate for that disparity, you have to make sure that the breathing you're doing is efficient, which means you have to breathe with your body organ that was designed to do it when speaking — your diaphragm. Your diaphragm is located beneath your lungs, so at first it will feel like you are breathing with your stomach, but anyone who's ever sung in a choir can attest to the results of sticking with it: you will get a fuller sound when breathing this way (as opposed to the shallower chest-breathing that most of us perform on a daily basis). If you're having difficulty getting the hang of this, lay down on your back and observe the rise and fall of your stomach; for some reason, it is easier to breathe from the diaphragm when lying completely prone. After getting the hang of how that feels, stand up and focus on breathing the same way, expanding and contracting your diaphragm rather than raising and lowering your chest and shoulders. Being aware of how and from where you're breathing will eventually become part of your routine; whenever you feel your shoulders rising, or that you're not getting quite enough air to project your voice as much as you'd like, pause. Get your breathing out of your lungs and shoulders and back down to your diaphragm where it belongs.

Another component of your voice is your pitch — the highness or lowness of its sound. Extremely high pitches, as well as extremely low, can be hard to listen to, and sometimes even to hear (especially true for the lower-pitched voice, for any amount of time). Most speakers' difficulty with pitch involves the high end of the spectrum because tension in the neck and shoulders can cause pitch to rise; sadly, a lot of people out there are carrying stress along with them in their neck and shoulders. In addition to working on breathing from your diaphragm, you may also wish to "relax your throat, jaw, and shoulders. You can do this by using simple neck and shoulder rolls and yawning to drop the jaw" (Antonelli 2000, 179–180).

Improving the pitch and volume of your voice is a task best addressed with a "practice makes perfect" attitude. Although you can practice with your actual speech points or text, I suggest choosing material that is both something you enjoy and something unrelated to your speech subject matter. Pick a book (I always head for Catherine's "my love for Heathcliff is like the eternal rocks below" monologue in *Wuthering Heights*) or a piece of poetry or a newspaper article that appeals to you, go into a room by yourself, close the door, and then read it to the walls. Simultaneously focus on your breathing. Practice taking your eyes off the text and looking at the audience (you'll have to use your imagination to turn the walls into a standing-room-only crowd) and give the text the four-star treatment. Another common problem with voice is the dreaded monotone, a by-product of being nervous. As we've already discovered, there really is no reason to be nervous, and if you find any part of the sentence you're reading interesting, give it a little added emphasis. If there are points to be made, list them carefully and tick them off on your fingers. Always be thinking, if you were sitting in the audience listening to you, what information would you want emphasized? Another common complaint directed at presenters is that they speak too fast, as if they are racing to the end;

most of us could probably retire if we had a dime for every time we've been told, either in a speech class or after a presentation of any sort, to "just slow down." I'm not saying that it's a bad pointer, I'm just saying that continually berating yourself only for speaking too fast may not be the best way to improve.

Above all, don't give up! Amazing things can be done with an instrument as versatile as the human voice, as evidenced by history: "In a clearing in the woods of the Green Mountains of Vermont there is a stone marker with an engraving commemorating that 'On July 7 and 8 in the year 1840, Daniel Webster spoke at this place to 15,000 people'" (Drucker 2000, 71). By spending some time listening to and experimenting with your voice, you'll stumble across your very own vocal style.

In addition to listening to your own voice, you will also want to be aware of your speaking stance. When speaking with friends or co-workers, how do you normally stand? Slouched, with your arms crossed? Are you most comfortable when leaning against something, or with perfect posture and both feet firmly braced planted on the ground? How do you stand when addressing a meeting room full of colleagues, or when meeting someone for the first time? What gestures do you use while speaking? For at least a day or so, try to quietly observe how you present yourself, physically, to others. What you'll be observing is your body (or nonverbal) behavior, which constitutes a large part of how your audience will perceive you. According to one of the pioneers in the field, Albert Mehrabian, "Nonverbal behavior refers to actions as distinct from speech. It thus includes facial expressions, hand and arm gestures, postures, positions, and various movements of the body or the legs and feet" (Mehrabian 1972, 1). Communication research has proven that audiences often judge a speaker's credibility and competence based on nonverbal factors such as eye contact, facial expression, and posture, so those are aspects of your style to which you will want to pay careful attention.

One of the fastest ways to feel confident is to appear confident, and this can easily be projected by your posture. Keeping your spine straight and rotating your shoulders back, keeping your head erect, and keeping your hands at your sides are all ways to improve your stance. Again, don't underestimate the value of arriving at your own nonverbal style. If you're comfortable standing behind a lectern, just make sure you do so without hiding behind it. If you like to talk with your hands, simply make sure that your gestures add something to your words and don't distract your listeners. Only after you stand up straight, smile, and make eye contact with the members of your audience should you worry about the words you're going to deliver using your pleasantly pitched and well-modulated voice.

Choose your words honestly and use them sparingly

In 1921, William Strunk wrote *The Elements of Style*, wherein he offered two very simple rules for effectively using language: "Use definite, specific, concrete language," and "Omit needless words." No matter how good the speaker or how useful the presentation, it's very rarely a sad occasion when a presentation is over (have you ever heard, "I love a finished speaker; oh, yes, indeed, I do. I don't mean one who's polished, I just mean one who's through"). Earlier it was suggested that you include more redundancy in your speeches than in your written communications, which seems an edict that is at odds with this one. However, the redundancy I advocated earlier was the repetition of your main points and topic for emphasis, not a suggestion that you repeat the same words over and over again for a longer amount of time — an important distinction.

Business literature (and other scholarly literature as well) often focuses on certain cultural differences and the various meanings of words in a global marketplace. Although you should always be aware of who is in your audience, your main consideration should nevertheless remain, "What is the simplest and best way to get my point(s) across?" regardless of concern for diversity and cultural differences. Sadly, there is no guarantee that anyone's vocabulary skills are as advanced as they could be: "In 1945, the average number of words in the written vocabulary of an American child age 6 to 14 was 25,000; by 1990, that number had dropped to 10,000" (Ruben 1998, 124).

In addition to using the simplest and the most appropriate words for every situation, it is also important that you minimize, wherever possible, your use of professional jargon. When I say jargon, I don't limit that to complicated terms such as "Values Based Circulation" and "Boolean operators"; a 1989 study of one hundred first-year students at Carnegie Mellon University noted that eighty-three percent of them (thankfully) knew what a call number was, but only sixty-eight percent knew what an online catalog was, and a mere thirty-five percent correctly defined *citation* (Naismith and Skein 1989, 548). If you're facing an audience you know will be com-fortable with the profession's jargon (you're not going to have to explain the acronym MARC to a roomful of catalogers, or BI to a roomful of teaching librarians), you may use it sparingly to save time, but don't use it to prove there's a reason you've been chosen to speak. As always, watching and responding to cues from your audience will be your best guide in your usage of jargon, and will be more fully explored in the next strategy.

Many times in the preparation of your speech, you will chance upon a phrase that you believe illustrates your point perfectly. Even if you don't write out your entire speech, you can cheat a little and write down any phrases or sentences that you'd really like to say just as you planned them. Those safety nets of nicely turned words and phrases should also provide a respectable confidence boost. After all, if your audience sees you using note cards or a short outline, they're not going to assume you have anything but the briefest of notes written on them, and will, no doubt, be all the more impressed with the gems you're tossing them "off the top of your head."

The average adult uses about five hundred words most often, and because each word has between twenty and twenty-five meanings, you've already got up to 12,500 possible meanings (Burley-Allen 1995, 65), so always make an effort to utilize the simplest and most effective words possible. That precept will serve you equally well whether you are teaching an introductory library course to a group of ESL (English as a Second Language) students, or giving a training presentation to the lawyers at the firm for which you're the special librarian. Keep your words short, keep them simple, and unless warranted by the subject (when I give book talks about rural fiction and nonfiction, I tend to get roused because of my farm upbringing and revert to some country colloquialisms), try to keep the slang and the jargon to a minimum. It is often said that a true professional makes doing something look easy; simple words are easy to use and easy to understand, and using them well will make you look like the true professional you are.

Observe your audience and adjust your tone and pace to them

Aristotle's *Rhetoric* is fairly straightforward in its assertion that the audience is the important component of the speaking equation: "For of the three elements in speech-making — speaker, subject, and person addressed — it is the last one, the hearer, that determines the speech's end and object" (Aristotle 1954, 32). It's all very nice that you've been asked (or told) to stand up in front of them, but in the end, they are the ones who matter, and their understanding of you and your topic will often dictate how you feel about a presentation, and whether or not you are ever asked to repeat it. It doesn't take a psychologist to notice when people look confused, or unhappy, or bored; all it takes is an attentive speaker who knows how to respond appropriately to those and other feedback cues provided free of charge by the audience.

First things first: make sure that you can be heard. If you are comfortable point-blank asking everyone in the back if they can hear you, that's fine, but a less confrontational way to accomplish that is to start by introducing yourself and your subject and carefully watching that back row while you do so; if they strain their heads toward you or lean forward, chances are they can't hear you. Make an effort to project your voice or move closer to your audience; it is permissible to move around while speaking, and it's often a good way to help your voice project toward the back as well as circulate amidst the front rows in an approachable manner. Depending on your venue and audience, you can also place yourself in the most advantageous position; if you're in a meeting room, take a middle seat at the conference table rather than one at the end; or if there isn't a table, consider moving the chairs, if possible, into a semicircular pattern.

The same logic applies when making sure that you are keeping pace with your audience, or, more precisely, whether your audience can keep pace with you. If you often observe your listeners still writing notes after you've moved on to a new subject, or that they are very rarely looking at you because they are so busy writing, you may wish to slow down just a bit. You may not be able to fit in everything you have planned to include, but you will have the satisfaction of knowing that, at least, your audience has absorbed what you did cover. Conversely, if people are looking around the room or showing other signs of a general lack of attention, you may be moving too slowly or repeating yourself unnecessarily. Make an effort to move on to your next point, and be sure to put some enthusiasm into your voice as you do so.

Another often-suggested but little-followed piece of advice is to initiate and maintain eye contact with your audience. That does not mean simply looking up from your notes and focusing on some imaginary point on the back wall;

my brother still regularly mocks his high school math teacher who never let his eyes wander below an imaginary line he had drawn one foot down from the ceiling and around the perimeter of the room. Start the process early on by speaking to or at least making some minimal contact with members of your audience when they enter the room. A simple "good morning" or smile or nod to your participants while distributing your handouts will give the impression of an open and interested speaker; continue that contact by smiling at members of your audience while speaking, and actually looking into their eyes.

Maintaining eye contact does not mean you have to stare at anyone. Marjorie Brody, a communication skills trainer, advises holding eye contact for approximately three to five seconds within a small group, and, when speaking to larger groups, beginning your eye contact with "people in the back corners of the room, which tend to be neglected. Hold your contact longer — perhaps zero to twenty-five seconds. Everyone in the general area will think you're looking at them" (Brody 1998, 29). In addition to creating a connection between you and your audience, the effective use of eye contact can also minimize distractions and audience member disruptions; public speaking coach Victoria Chorbajian offers a tip for addressing someone in your audience who is talking: "Focus eye contact directly on her until she stops. This shows you are in control and gets the audience to focus entirely on you" (Eye Contact 1998, 80).

All of the skills just considered should be common knowledge but are not often used to their full advantage. Jo-Ellan Dimitrius and Mark Mazzarella discuss these, and many other techniques for observing other people, in their book *Reading People: How to Understand People and Predict Their Behavior — Anytime, Anyplace.* Although you should not have to read entire books on how to read your audience, keep their advice in mind: "What is their body language telling you? Are eyes rolling? Is there eye contact? Are there signs of boredom or attentiveness? Are they coming closer to you or moving farther away?" (Dimitrius and Mazzarella 1998, 251). Noticing those cues is what sets good observers and speakers apart from poor and uninteresting ones.

Review your speech mentally immediately after giving it

Obviously you may not be able to seek seclusion immediately after you finish speaking, but you should make a habit of taking a few quiet minutes to yourself, as soon as possible, to review your performance intellectually and critique it. Before snatching those few minutes for yourself, however, devote some time to remaining accessible to your listeners; many times people will have follow-up questions for you that they may not have been comfortable asking in front of others, or simply hadn't thought of until the present moment. There is usually some kind of tidying up or straightening of the room you can perform while you remain behind as your audience departs; teaching librarians can shut down the computers in the lab, meeting facilitators can push the chairs in around the conference table, and public librarians can return their room to order after a book talk or other presentation. By performing these small tasks, you not only do something necessary, but you remain available for your audience. Thank them for coming as they leave and, if anyone wants to chat with you afterward, recognize and take advantage of a great opportunity to learn something or to speak more personally with individuals. Only after you have exhausted this valuable source of relaxation and feedback should you seek a few moments of solitude.

Ask yourself questions that reflect those you considered while preparing your presentation:

✓ Did you get through your main points?

✓ Was your introduction successful in obtaining your audience's attention?

✓ Were your handouts well-received, and did your participants take them along when leaving?

✓ Did your audience give you body language cues that indicated interest or confusion?

✓ Did anyone ask questions, or introduce an aspect of the topic that you hadn't previously thought of?

✓ Were you happy with the summarizing value of your conclusion, and did you have the time to present it?

By the time you have answered those and the other questions that might occur to you as you review your performance, you will know what to change in order to improve your next presentation. If your jokes were not well-received you may want to skip the joke and go with a short story or anecdote instead. If you saw a lot of blank stares by the time you got to your last point, you may have been trying to cover too much, or perhaps you covered the point too quickly. Briefly relive your talk, even if it's one you never

intend to give again, and ask yourself how you could have improved it. Then, go one step further, and make a note of things you did do effectively. Such a review is a form of practice in which I believe much more strongly than endlessly reciting your talk to an empty room ahead of time. Once your colleagues and patrons learn you're willing to give presentations, you'll most likely receive more speaking requests, and every presentation you give will make you a stronger and better speaker. Practice based on the idea of review will also help you evaluate which aspects of the situation were within your control and which ones weren't. A tour of the library may go off without a hitch one day, with you remembering every aspect of the library you're showing off as well as every fun fact you wanted to regale your group with, but the same tour the next day may be a miserable experience — just because you have to give it after lunch when everyone's drowsy, or you have to give it the minute after you get to work in a rainstorm, while you're still wet and a little out of sorts. A truly proficient speaker never really stops preparing for that next presentation, and the easiest and optimal time to start that preparation is directly after giving one, when your audience's reactions and questions are still fresh in your mind.

Chapter Summary

How you sound and how you look while you address an audience are two of the main variables that determine whether or not they will find you credible, enthusiastic, and enjoyable to listen to. Using your voice to its fullest potential (both in volume and in pitch) by breathing efficiently and with your diaphragm, and using your posture and body language to project a positive and confident image are two ways to ensure that your speech merits your and your audience's time. It is also important that you employ simple and clear language, and that you avoid superfluous jargon and inappropriate slang.

Although you may feel overburdened by the task of simultaneously monitoring your voice, stance, and word choice, you must never forget to monitor your listeners, or to watch for the feedback cues that indicate whether or not they are hearing and understanding you. When your presentation is over and you've restored the room or hall or corner to its original state and answered last-minute questions or concerns, take a moment to review your speech performance mentally, as well as to write down suggestions or reminders for future engagements.

In one chapter we've traveled more than two thousand years, from Aristotle, who reluctantly reminds us that our delivery is important, to communication professor Stephen Lucas, who admonishes that "to be an effective speaker, you must be audience-centered.... You cannot assume that listeners will be interested in what you have to say" (Lucas 1998, 19). Nor can you assume that they'll be interested in discussing any of what you have to say with you or their co-participants, which is why the next chapter addresses methods for encouraging audience participation and discussion.

CHAPTER 6

Discussion and Participation

Students' questions can turn into the life of the party.
— Donald A. Barclay, *Teaching Electronic Information Literacy*

All public speaking textbooks and how-to articles agree on one thing: talking with your audience is vastly preferable to talking at them. Initiating and encouraging discussion and participation effectively instantly makes any presentation more enjoyable and useful for both the speaker and the participants. I'll admit it; I don't believe in reading speeches from prepared scripts, because that denies you the possibility of interaction and spontaneity. If you go into a presentation prepared to cover your main points but still open to the questions and suggestions the audience can provide for you, you will have set the stage for a mutually beneficial conversation.

If you are a teaching librarian, what would you rather do? Give the same instructional presentation, with no variations, thirty times in a row, or learn or consider something new in thirty different and vibrant class sessions? You wouldn't dream of setting out to bore your audience, so why inflict that same punishment upon yourself?

We Answer Questions for a Living — Why Be Scared of Them While Speaking?

Encouraging audience participation can be scary because a number of different fears are involved with facilitating question-and-answer sessions. Dorothy Leeds, author of the very popular book *Powerspeak*, lists a number of them: "[worry that] you lose control when you open the floor to questions, you will get a question you are not prepared for, or you will have to answer whatever questions come along" (Leeds 1991, 197). It can also be scary, because according to Mary Jane Scherdin's recent study of librarian personality types, "Sixty-three percent of librarians have Introverted preferences" (Scherdin 1994, 108), which may make it particularly hard for many of us to be as outgoing as it is often necessary to be when conversing with an audience. So, comfortably interacting with others can be one of the hardest fears to overcome, but that high learning curve also ensures that anyone who masters these skills will be even more valuable as a speaker and employee.

I highly encourage conquering what may be your natural tendency to avoid confrontation with your audience, not only because it will be professionally beneficial to you, but also because, put quite simply, every moment you can encourage an audience member to speak is another moment that you don't have to. The easiest ways to become proficient in discussion and question facilitation are to employ a definite plan of action, observe your audience in order to encourage and respond to their contributions, spend some of your work time reading about communication theories and discussion tactics, and always ask your audience for their opinions after your presentation.

Have a plan

I realize that by now you may be tired of hearing about this strategy over and over again, but being prepared is really the proper approach to any speaking engagement. You have already invested a lot time in your research, in developing your main points, and in preparing your introduction and conclusion. Don't make the mistake of assuming that you cannot anticipate and plan for the wild card of audience input. If you go in with the expectation that no matter what comes up, you will be the leader of the situation, you'll be able to respond effectively to anything your audience can throw at you. It's always a good idea to have a backup plan, whether it's in case your "live" presentation encounters problems, or your PowerPoint slides won't open, or your initial plan for getting input from your audience doesn't work. Planning to ask your audience an open-ended question during the introduction to earn their interest is a good idea, and having the confidence to ask a specific person in the audience for an answer to that question when no one volunteers is an even better one. If your audience doesn't respond to your first question, plan on having the courage to allow a moment of silence while they think about it, and then rephrase the question and request nicely that someone answer it for you.

One underestimated facilitation technique is to allow for silences and pauses after you've posed a question or issue for discussion. For example, one research study found that when teachers paused for three seconds (instead of one) after a student's response, the average length of responses increased from seven words (after a one-second pause) to twenty-eight words (Hargie 1994, 117). Usually you have to go after success, but sometimes you really can sit back and wait for it. Pausing or allowing slight moments of silence after your questions or participants' responses—although it may feel like an eternity—can provide the time your audience needs to formulate more complete thoughts and questions.

In addition to allowing pauses and moments of silence, there are a number of ways to plan for and encourage audience response:

✓ Ask them a question and have them answer as a group, or individually.

✓ Give a demonstration and encourage the audience to question your procedures.

✓ Play devil's advocate or use startling statements or facts to elicit strong reactions.

✓ Share a personal anecdote or experience, and provide an opportunity for them to do the same.

✓ Ask your audience to do something; raise their hands in response, perform a certain action in the database or program you're teaching, stand (or sit) in response to a query, etc.

✓ Inform them of what you'd like them to do and why ("I need one member of every group to record your group's thoughts, and another member of the group to volunteer for sharing those thoughts with everyone when we reconvene, so we can hear a variety of the groups' ideas").

The more intricate your discussion ideas, the more carefully you have to anticipate and plan. If you are facilitating a meeting or conference session, and want people to discuss very specific topics in small groups, you must do more than say, "Okay, everyone work with the people at your table to talk about these issues." You must move about among the participants, not only helping them form specific groups, but perhaps listening momentarily to the discussion or even joining in the conversation briefly before moving on. Provide writing materials for them if you have asked them to take notes or record any results. Don't be afraid to assign very specific topics, or to ask the groups to state their conclusions to the larger assembly. Set a time limit for what you want to achieve (three ideas per group, one procedural checklist, and so forth.) and abide by it. When that time limit is reached, respectfully demand the attention of your audience, and be sure to hear everyone's contributions. Dorothy Leeds's *Powerspeak* book is still in print largely because it encourages you, as the speaker, to take and keep control. Nowhere is that suggestion more useful than when encouraging group participation and communication.

Observe and respond to your audience appropriately

Teaching librarians can often get responses by simply calling on a member of the audience for a suggestion or answer; one of the librarians interviewed for this book actually mentioned doing so as one of her favorite parts of speaking: "Sometimes from students, you know, when you're doing a MadCat [OPAC] workshop or something, in those cases, then I usually just point at people, and say 'How about you?' Especially the people that are falling asleep in the back, or whatever they're doing in the back, not paying attention, I love to say, 'You in the hat, what would you say?' It's amazing how the rest of them will perk up" (Grow 2002). That is one of the more intimidating methods for everyone involved, speaker and spoken to, but observing your audience carefully will help you use it tactfully and effectively. Again, you do not have to be a psychologist to notice which students in your audience appear to be more comfortable contributing. The goal here is not to arbitrarily make people uncomfortable or fearful of being put on the spot, but rather to indicate that all input is welcome, and that in exchange for your trying to give the best presentation possible, you expect your audience to do the best listening possible. In any room of students or workshop attendees there will always be someone who doesn't mind answering any question put to them, and you can find those people easily by initiating eye contact with your audience members and taking note of who returns it. Even participants who sit in the back row (forgive the generalization) and never look up at you will notice that the people you're calling on have not perished from failure or embarrassment, and as the session progresses, may even look up and start to signal their own willingness to participate.

For those of you not teaching high school or college students, starting discussions amongst other groups of people and colleagues can be much easier (another librarian I spoke to indicated that her difficulty facilitating participation arose from people wanting to talk too much), although our profession still consists overwhelmingly of people who are too quick to assume that they have nothing to offer.

In meetings, in conference workshops, in public library programs, in corporate information center training sessions, you will often find yourself facing audiences who are more than willing to discuss their opinions and questions with you and with others. Your task then becomes one of mediation, and the need for observing your audience becomes, if anything, even greater.

There are many types of personalities and communicators, and in an open forum, those who are less shy about expounding on their opinions will often, inadvertently or not, dominate the discussion. It is your task to watch eyes and faces, as well as body language, to learn when someone is confused or in disagreement with the points being offered, and further, it is your job to subtly encourage them to voice those opinions. In situations like that you can begin with an open-ended question, such as, "Does anyone think there might be another approach to this issue?" That question indicates your willingness to hear other points of view. In extreme cases you may directly address those you suspect have something to contribute, but often simply validating differences of opinion with such open questions is sufficient to encourage people to talk.

Although you must be ready with both a plan and a backup plan for eliciting responses, it is also important to avoid the belief that there is only one correct or appropriate answer or reaction to your questions. Donald A. Barclay addresses that issue in his book on teaching information literacy: "Rarely, if ever, will you extract the identical answer you have contrived. Be willing to use the terms and partially correct answers elicited from the class to rephrase and clarify the answer" (Barclay 1995, 30).

Devote time to learning about communication theories and discussion tactics

Every profession has more than its fair share of theory and research, and there is no shortage of literature on communication theories, library science, or the two combined. Although many of you may well be too busy just keeping up with your daily workload, devoting a bit of time to background reading on the science of interacting with an audience is never time wasted. Consider the following tidbits of information:

✓ When volunteers were asked to rate the competence of communicators with low eye contact and with high eye contact, the competence ratings were significantly higher for the subjects who exhibited high eye contact with the audience (Fatt 1999, 38).

✓ In some Asian cultures, direct eye contact is considered rude (Brody 1998, 29).

✓ Women in conversation spend much more time looking at each other (referred to as "mutual gaze") than do men; thirty-eight percent to twenty-three percent, respectively (Ingram 1992, 10).

✓ The most common discussion monopolizer is the teacher; in a typical discussion class the teacher talked seventy to eighty percent of the time (McKeachie 1999, 57).

✓ "Audiences tend to perceive women who do not appear confident in front of people as lacking ability. A less than confident or uncomfortable man, however, may be perceived as endearing, particularly by a female audience" (Bienvenu 2000, 141).

Those are all pieces of information that might conceivably help you in a future presentation, and most were easily found with a five-minute search and subject browse through a basic abstracting database. As a librarian, you occupy the enviable position of having more and better access to more sources of information than most professionals; use that access and your expertise to continually learn as much as possible about the subject of communication.

Remember what you've read or file away the more helpful hints in a tickler file, one you could read when you have a little extra time at the reference desk, or before you have to head out to a conference to give a talk.

If possible, get feedback from your audience after your presentation

The possibility of eliciting feedback from your audience will vary widely depending upon who your audience is, and what the purpose of the presentation was. For many teaching librarians, official evaluation surveys are provided and often required for the purposes of keeping statistics, whereas a public or children's librarian may not have the formalized resources available for such quantifiable results. You will have to assess each speaking encounter individually and do what is most appropriate under the circumstances to gather audience response.

You may wish to think of this step as your introduction in reverse; just as it can be calming to get to know your listeners by chatting with them beforehand, it can be very helpful to stay late and do the same thing to achieve a slightly different purpose. Many times, if you have given a program at a public library, a convention, or in the community, members of your audience will approach you afterward with questions or comments they have regarding your topic. That is, hands down, the best source of material for your next such presentation. Their questions can serve as reminders of information you may have inadvertently left out (or did not have the time to cover), or as indicators of aspects of your subject matter that your audience might have interest in but that have not occurred to you.

You can always also hope for those superlative audience members who not only offer opinions or compliments on your subject, but also other observations on your presentation style itself. Those comments can either be great for your self-esteem and confidence in your speaking skills (if they're compliments) or at least provide very constructive criticism for your next talk ("I really liked what you had to say, but it was hard to hear you at all times").

Colleagues can also be a rich source of audience support and feedback. I once attended a meeting with my supervisor, and was both flattered and impressed when she asked me afterward if there were any aspects of her speaking style that I thought she could have improved to make the meeting more worthwhile for everyone involved. Take a friend or a co-worker along to your next presentation and ask him or her to honestly critique your performance afterward. Everybody has a unique speaking style, and combining the best parts of yours with the sincere suggestions of others can help you hybridize the most effective way for you to communicate.

The opportunities for this kind of feedback are many; even if you work in an environment with fewer librarian colleagues on staff (many times, special librarians and school librarians are employed in smaller departments or as the only information professional), you can be creative in your solicitation of feedback. If you work for a company, you may have regular reviews with the staff human resources person, or if you work in a school, you may often interact with the teachers or school administration. Let them know that you take your communications skills (and their improvement) very seriously, and that you expect them to do so as well. Human resources specialists are educated in interpersonal relationships and communication, and simply letting them know you would appreciate their expertise

should be sufficient to elicit some kind of response.

If the situation allows and it falls to you to create official feedback survey or comment cards, give careful thought to their design and wording. If it's your responsibility to facilitate a focus group on any aspect of your library's product or services, spend some time researching focus group design and facilitation. Some rules of thumb for scientific feedback collection include, but are not limited to, these guidelines:

✓ Use clear, simple, and unambiguous wording.

✓ Keep the form or focus group meeting as short as possible to encourage your audience to complete the entire form or session.

✓ If using numerical scales for audience satisfaction measurement, make sure the scales are explained fully and clearly labeled.

✓ Always leave space or time for an invitation to your audience to comment on *any* aspect of your presentation, product, or services.

Chapter Summary

When you make the commitment to give a presentation, you should not only want to make the presentation effective, but you should also have a bit of fun doing so. A recent television commercial showed little kids spilling all sorts of their mothers' secrets to a relative (the ad was for chewy granola bars, presumably helpful to keep youngsters' jaws busy). That's funny not only because we can relate to it, but because a lot of the world's laughs are based on what people can and do say in any given situation. Don't miss out on the best part of speaking to people, which is encouraging them to speak with one another and with you.

Although it can be challenging to overcome your fear of interacting more directly with your audience, it is a challenge you can easily meet by taking the time to plan your discussion techniques, observing your audience and reacting to their reactions appropriately, researching communication and participation theories, and always asking for evaluation of your skills by colleagues, audience members, and yourself.

PART TWO
The Speaking Environment

CHAPTER 7

Interviewing

Next to public speaking, most people think that enduring a job interview is one of the most stressful human experiences.
— Richard Koonce, "How to Ace a Job Interview"

A recent search of the Library Literature database on the terms "job?" and "interview?" retrieved 35 article hits for the years 1985 through 2001. A comparable search in ABI Inform (a business database) for the past two years alone retrieved 525 articles. ABI Inform is a bigger and broader database, and interviewing tactics are a huge issue for those in business and human resources professionals, but that huge disparity still seems indicative of the lack of importance attached to developing interviewing skills within our profession.

It is ironic that the great bulk of the research done in library schools every year is on the subject of the *reference* interview. When it comes to attempting to help others, the interest of librarians is rampant; when it comes to helping ourselves, we don't pay the least bit of attention.

Interviews are tough. Even seasoned and extroverted professionals sometimes have difficulty negotiating them well, which is evidenced by the many, many journal articles and books specifically addressing that subject. In a world where library schools are struggling to answer the question "Are librarians necessary in the age of the Internet?" and where growth in the field's employment opportunities has slowed considerably, it is more important that we stop assuring ourselves that we're necessary and instead concentrate on convincing others of our value.

Contrary to popular belief, I don't think the problem is exclusively one of image, but rather one of failing to develop our skills (including proficiency in public speaking) and using them to get the jobs we deserve.

So the logical question is, how can a group of people who overwhelmingly display introverted tendencies put their best feet forward in the most stressful of social and business situations? The answer is to maximize our profession's specialized skills while learning to portray our weaknesses, if not inversely as strengths, at least as recognized characteristics that can make us more aware of the difficulties of others.

Being All That You Can Be: It's Not Just for the Army Anymore

I would like to tell interviewees that they should just be themselves and trust their own style, but the smallest amount of reading in human resources and interviewing literature has provided me with a slightly reworked suggestion: be the best you that you can be. Before you express disgust at the jingoistic ring of that idea, stop and think about it. Millions of dollars are spent on interview question-and-answer books and resources each year, but most of the information expounded in them will only teach you how to be the best *generic* job applicant you can be. Anyone can tell an interviewer that his or her only weakness is a tendency to work too hard and put in too many hours, but how many interviewers actually believe that?

The true prowess lies in answering the questions well, and giving solid reasons for your answers while still being true to your personality. Cover letters and résumés exist to project whether or not you are qualified for the position; the interview helps determine whether you will be a good fit for the organization (professionally and personally), and perhaps even more importantly, whether the organization will be a good fit for you. The interview gives your potential employer the opportunity to try to hire the best and most appropriate staff member possible, but it also gives you the opportunity to discern whether with the organization will provide colleagues you can work with productively as well as a suitable work environment. To that end, honesty regarding your personality is imperative on your part, just as an hon-est portrayal of the work environment is on the company's part. Oftentimes individuals dislike interviewing job candidates even more than they dislike being interviewed, and are therefore not in a hurry to hire more often than necessary. That reality alone should prompt you to consider any means available to improve your interview performance. Let's turn to some of those possibilities now by examining this often-dreaded but very useful interaction, step by step.

The Process of Interviewing

Research

As a librarian, you are ideally and uniquely qualified to research the organization or company with whom you hope to obtain an interview. Those of you seeking jobs as special or corporate librarians will want to do the requisite company research on their finances, SEC filings, growth rate, and other such related characteristics, so that you can provide answers that complement the company's mission and goals. If you haven't already, you'll also want to perform broader research on industry trends and other business happenings in your chosen field. If, for example, you'll be applying at a credit union, you'll want to be well versed in all recent banking news and trends. If applying at a law firm, you will not only need to know legal research methods but also the firm's specific areas of practice and any special considerations attached to them.

Those librarians hoping to work in public or academic libraries need to be very familiar with the institution's mission statement and stated long-term goals. Regardless of your opinion of "mission" or "vision" statements per se, you can assume that someone at the organization, if not entire groups of people, took a lot of time and deliberation in developing them, and it's the best clue you're likely to get about a library's areas of concentration and specification. Familiarize yourself with the institution's mission, and after making sure that it corresponds with your own vision of what you want to get out of the job and, of course, contribute to it, spend some time thinking about how you will present yourself as an able partner in making their statement viable. Academic librarians will want to acquaint themselves with the institution's tenure requirements and process and their subject matter; school librarians will want to learn something about their school district's policies and statistics; public librarians will want to learn the logistics of the neighborhood in which the library is located and the system's goals and statistics; and freelance editorial professionals and information brokers will obviously be wise to spend some time looking at the publisher's catalog and output or the company's balance sheet and outside research needs.

The many variations and possibilities for pre-interview research are too numerous to list here, but just as in any other presentation, you should get to know your topic and your audience, which, in this case, means doing a substantial amount of background research.

Appearance and Introductions

Career coach and professional speaker Richard Koonce places in perspective the importance of first impressions at interviews when he states:

"Eighty percent of the first impression an interviewer gets of you is visual — and it's formed in the first two minutes of the meeting" (Koonce 1997, 13). Because librarians and other information professionals are involved in such a wide variety of work environments and corporate cultures, it is impossible to set down one hard-and-fast rule for dressing appropriately for any particular interview. Dress codes are often informally disseminated and enforced, and are therefore hard to research ahead of time, but there are a few rules of thumb that can be used to determine the most suitable attire. If your interview is being scheduled through human resources, feel to ask about dress code requirements and interview expectations; it's that department's job to know those types of things and provide that information to employees. If at all possible, visit your potential workplace briefly and try to surreptitiously observe the dress code. If neither of those possibilities are an option, follow the advice of an interview expert and "dress the best you're ever going to look in the job you want" (Kennedy 2000, 78).

Other aspects of making the best first impression possible are easily obtained from the Internet and also from books aimed at a more general market. For the purposes of this book, I'll go out on a limb and assume you know enough about getting a job to avoid such errors as wearing provocative, wrinkled, or soiled clothing, or flashy jewelry. Just the other day I happened to catch a snippet of the TV game show *Family Feud*, when they gave the top three answers to their Internet interactive question: "What shouldn't you do in a job interview?" The first two answers were standard fare (don't be late, don't wear sloppy clothes), but it was the third reply I really enjoyed: don't swear. So, and I have it now on *Family Feud* authority, don't swear.

One small aspect of making a good first impression that I would like to discuss is the introductory handshake. A counseling specialist at the University of Texas at Dallas compiled a rating of applicant behaviors from a study of job recruiters, and a "firm handshake" was rated a 4 on a scale of 5 (with 5 being "very important"), directly between "knowledge of employer," which ranked 4.1, and "good posture," at 3.9 (Kennedy 2000, 75). I had the opportunity to learn the importance of a good handshake in a high school drama class. Our teacher introduced us to a theater professional she knew, and when I shook his hand, he asked my teacher why all her students "shook hands like wet fish." With my feelings immediately hurt, I attempted a stronger handshake with him and was then told, "Don't just squeeze harder." His first lesson to all of us, right then, was to make us practice shaking hands with our classmates until we had developed a firm handshake, meeting one another's outstretched hands fully (placing the base of our thumbs together to avoid simply squeezing each other's fingers). I've never forgotten that day (along with typing, it's one of the few skills I can thank my high school education for) and have been pleasantly surprised that potential employers (as well as anyone you're being introduced to) are so easily impressed by a firm and steady handshake. Try not to worry about your sweaty palms; keep your fingers open before a handshake and the air reaching your palm will eradicate most of that problem. Other characteristics listed by recruiters as impressive included "enthusiasm" and "communication skills,"

numbers one and two, respectively (Kennedy 2000, 75).

Remember that if you can successfully navigate those first two minutes, most of which is largely filled with introductions, smiles, and handshakes, you've done eighty percent of the work of creating a good first impression. Use the confidence gained from that good start to decrease your nervousness and focus your attention on the next part of the interview.

Answering Questions

For the most part, answering questions is what librarians do for a living, so we find ourselves once again uniquely qualified, though often under-practiced, in answering questions in a situation as fraught with tension as the job interview. Remember, if you already have a job in a library, it may be easy for you to obtain a book on sample interview questions and answers, and you probably already have the skills necessary to perform other supplementary research. Don't discount the usefulness of those skills; I can assure you that a large amount of my time behind the public library's reference desk involves helping *other* people find books on writing résumés and answering interview questions, as well as helping them research the companies for which they hope to work.

If you don't have the time or the desire to consult a reference book on stereotypical interview questions, prepare as you normally would for any presentation in which you might expect a lot of questions from your audience: know your subject matter, and try to remain calm and collected while facing your querier. Most interviewers will not fault you for pausing to carefully consider your answer before you reply, and many will actively approve of your doing so, because it indicates that you are listening carefully and striving to answer the questions to the best of your ability. Don't let your nerves compel you to just start rambling rather than allowing a moment of silence; instead, take a deep breath, look the interviewer in the eye, and answer the question honestly and succinctly.

As much as you may try to anticipate or prepare for an interviewer's questions, it is impossible to predict with any certainty exactly which questions you will be asked. A friend of mine who recently started interviewing for his first professional position was ecstatic when he chanced upon what he thought was a spectacular answer to the question "What is your greatest weakness?" (His answer: a lack of proficiency in foreign languages, which he was trying to improve by studying Spanish). Imagine his disappointment when the question failed to come up in any of his multiple interviews! Likewise, although many career guides and manuals will suggest surefire ways to answer stereotypical questions such as "Tell us about yourself" or "Where do you see yourself in five years?" their answers will probably not be as interesting or as beneficial as your own honest and unambiguous answers. It's not that there isn't anything to be learned from books that promise to decode standard interview questions for you, but before memorizing answers to questions you may not even be asked, you might wish to sit down and prepare for your interview in the same manner you would for any other presentation or program: write out your main points in an outline and give a little thought to what your audience might like to take away from your meeting.

For example, if you have applied for a job as a law librarian, your main points would most likely fall into a logical pattern of the following items:

✓ Your education.

✓ Your unique work qualifications.

✓ Your interest in one particular firm over another.

Under those points you can list the appropriate information: your master's of library science and law degrees, your employment history during your education or your previous professional positions (depending on where you are in your career), and your particular interest in the firm you are interviewing with because of its focus on, say, adoption law. If you don't enjoy thinking of unique or attention-grabbing introductions, preparing for speaking at an interview will probably be easier than for other presentations. All you need to get a potential employer's attention is your enthusiasm and a willingness to talk with everyone involved in interviewing you. The same goes for your conclusion, with the caveat that one thing you may wish to prepare in advance is a number of questions for those final interview moments when any good interviewer will ask if *you* have any questions.

If you are usually more comfortable writing your presentations out in their entirety ahead of time, you could also write out a short, all-purpose paragraph that highlights your accomplishments and shows a willingness to improve whatever might be construed as your weaknesses. As with preparing other speeches, I would advise that you not be too tied to the exact wording. Interviews are stressful enough without trying to recite from memory "canned" (both in preparation and tone) lists of your attributes. Far better to prepare and review an outline of your skills and qualifications before an interview, and take your time to visualize it during your interview.

Asking Questions

If you're applying for a reference librarian position, asking good questions of your interviewers can be a great way to prove both your research skills and your ability to ask relevant questions (excellent attributes for someone working the reference desk). If the job you're applying for is not a reference position, however, you will still wish to have some questions ready in advance for potential employers, even though you may think of additional and perhaps more specific questions during the interview.

Show your interviewers that your interest in the position is such that you took the time to study their organization or company, and to formulate some questions that would increase your understanding of the work environment, the job itself, and your potential place in the organization. Nothing is worse than not having anything to say when an employer asks, "Do you have any questions for us?" Ask your questions, listen carefully to the answers, and don't be afraid to ask follow-up questions. At the same time that you are presenting yourself to your interviewer(s), he/she/they are presenting themselves to you as well; make a note of how seriously your questions are taken and how well they are answered, and take that into consideration when deciding whether or not to accept the job if it is offered to you. Your first few months at a new job will consist largely of learning by asking questions, so you'll want to make

sure you're getting involved with a group of colleagues who are amenable to answering your questions, and who do so well.

After the Interview

Any good librarian knows that having all of the information available leads to the best decision making, and you should take steps to ensure that you have all the information you need about the position you've applied for, and also that your interviewer has learned everything necessary about you. Don't be afraid to politely ask questions such as "When do you anticipate you'll be making your decision and contacting applicants?" or any variation thereof. After all, if you're applying for one job, you're probably applying and interviewing for several, concurrently, and knowing when one employer plans to finalize a hiring decision can help you organize your responses and ultimately, your acceptance of a position. Any form of that question also shows your continued interest in the position, much as the typical statement "I look forward to discussing this position further with you, and invite you to contact me at your earliest convenience" does in your cover letters. Ask your questions, thank your interviewer, and use the final interview moments to display your more friendly and outgoing professional style, as well as to invite your interviewer to contact you if further questions arise.

Never assume that the interview has ended when you walk out the door. First impressions may be the most important, but second impressions, in the form of your follow-up behavior, are also very important. After you've finished the interview and made a few short notes to yourself about what went well and what didn't (don't forget those short notes you should make immediately after any presentation) and be sure to send an e-mail or regular mail thank-you letter. For those of you who find writing thank-you letters as painful as writing tailored cover letters, remember to keep it simple and fast. Thank the interviewer for meeting with you, reiterate your desire to have them contact you with any further questions, and if you know you left out any important information during the interview (which the notes you took afterward will help you determine), include it now. Write the letter quickly, proofread it carefully, and send it within twenty-four hours of your interview. If nothing else, a letter is simply an easy way to keep your name in front of your interviewer(s); after the interviews, they will gather to rank the candidates they've spoken to, and it certainly isn't going to hurt you to impress your name and your interest in the position upon them one last time. Although most human resource professionals used to encourage a follow-up phone call, they are now shifting toward the opinion that an e-mail or letter follow-up is more effective because it allows employers to receive and read your additional thoughts at their convenience. If, however, you have not heard the outcome of the job interview by the date your interviewer(s) suggested a decision would be reached, feel free to make a polite phone inquiry regarding the status of the position.

Special Types of Interviews

The Phone Interview

Although it has often made my parents sigh with dismay, my tendency to look for a new job every few years has provided me with a lot of different interviewing experiences. I can safely say that the worst interview I've ever had, in terms of being both unsuccessful and painful, was a phone interview for a part-time public librarian position. It honestly couldn't have gone any worse if I had actively tried to fail, and I think I can safely tell you why: I was embarrassingly under-prepared for it. Always treat phone interviews with the respect they deserve, and do not underestimate their importance. Just because your interviewer(s) can't see you doesn't mean you should casually pick up the phone wearing your bathrobe and without having done every bit as much research and preparation as you would for a face-to-face interview. If anything, you should prepare more: when you're on the phone, you can't rely on your smile, handshake, posture, and nonverbal expressions of interest and enthusiasm to help you out, and so you must focus on speaking well and knowing your material. The sole advantage to a phone interview is that you may be able to structure your environment so that some of the preparation you did is accessible to you. Take the call at a desk or table, and have information regarding your qualifications, information about the company or organization, and your questions spread out before you. Dress the part and use your best possible phone voice (see chapter 8), and don't let any pauses or the sound of taking notes from the other end of the line unnerve you. It is hard to make personal connections with people when you cannot make eye contact, but do strive to use your best voice and posture, and if it helps you, gesture as you would if your interviewer could see you. Always make sure you completely understand a question before you answer it; again, take your time and a deep breath before providing your response.

The Interview Presentation

Because giving presentations and speeches is becoming a larger part of everyone's work duties, particularly in the library and information science fields, you may be asked to prepare and give a short presentation to your interviewer(s) as part of the meeting. A study of employment recruiters recently published in *Business Communication Quarterly* found that "the top five skills sought [in applicants], not unexpectedly, are 1. communication (oral and written); 2. computer literacy; 3. interpersonal/social; 4. critical thinking/leadership (tied); and 5. teamwork" (Moody 2002, 21). Rather than being nervous or intimidated by a request to give a presentation, use it as an opportunity to showcase your oral communication skills and differentiate yourself from the other job candidates. If you prepare your talk using the methods discussed in the first half of this book, you should be well on your way to giving a great presentation, and there is no easier way to impress your future employer than to go into a tough situation (the interview) and use your communication skills to shine.

If you have been asked to give a presentation, there are a few things you can do to minimize the difficulties associated with such a task. When scheduling your interview time, ask at least the following pertinent questions:

✓ What should the presentation cover?

✓ How long should it be?

✓ How many people will I be addressing?

✓ Would you like me to prepare a talk using presentation software or a live Internet connection?

Those are all initial considerations that must be regarded before preparing your talk. If, during your preparations, you think of more questions, compile them as you go and call your interviewer for clarifications; but do make an effort to clear up any remaining issues with one phone call. Ask if the use of handouts or visual aids, if applicable, would be acceptable; ask if a more static performance or one that includes audience participation is preferable. Raising those types of questions will also demonstrate your command of the speaking environment and its many variables—another skill that is always beneficial to display.

The Other Side of the Desk: How to Be a Good Interviewer

Why is it important to you and your organization to interview position applicants as effectively as possible? One main reason is the price tag associated with making a bad decision. Hiring individuals who are not a good match for the environment (or vice versa) can lead to dissatisfied and unproductive employees, and eventually a high turnover rate, which means more hiring, additional training time, and higher costs. Those outlays can be significant; the U.S. Department of Labor estimates that it costs one-third of a new hire's annual salary to replace an employee (Camp 2001, 3).

The process of becoming a good interviewer is more analogous to becoming a good public speaker than to becoming a good interviewee. As the interviewer, it is assumed that you, more so than the applicant, are in control of the environment. You can positively affect the experience by following the same steps that you might use to prepare a presentation: develop active listening skills, carefully research and plan the open position's requirements and expectations, choose and familiarize yourself with the interview space, prepare an outline with your basic questions, and be ready to analyze the response of your interviewee. Additionally, if you are interviewing as part of a committee or in a group, it won't hurt to ask your colleagues how they feel the interview process, and your questions in particular, are being received and answered.

Chapter Summary

If studies of library research indicate anything, it's that librarians care far more about perfecting their reference interview skills than they do about improving their job interview skills. Although library science attracts professionals who may be more interested in working behind the scenes than they are in promoting their own skills and services, it is important to face job interviews with confidence and a specific plan of action. Always perform comprehensive research on the company or institution where you'd like to work, carefully plan your appearance and the introductions to make the best possible first impression, use your public speaking skills to thoroughly and sincerely answer and ask questions, and always follow up after your interview by sending either an e-mail or regular mail thank-you letter.

When faced with the prospect of being interviewed over the telephone, research your prospective employer thoroughly, assemble your research and personal information within easy reach of where you'll sit to take the call, and dress professionally and maintain good posture while on the telephone. When answering questions over a telephone line, you cannot depend on a smile or your gestures to imply your interest, so you must focus on speaking pleasantly and well, as well as enunciating clearly so your interviewer can understand you.

If you are asked to prepare a presentation to give before or after your scheduled interview, get the information you need to prepare the presentation fully. Ask the person who has contacted you to schedule the interview questions such as what topic you should address, what speaking tools and software you will be expected to use, and how many people you will be addressing.

Further Reading

Camp, Richaurd, et al., *Strategic Interviewing: How to Hire Good People*, Jossey-Bass, San Francisco, 2001. An excellent book outlining the approach of "strategic interviewing," which consists of such techniques as developing realistic goals for the interview process and using behavioral decision-making to predict the candidate's performance on the job. If you'll be interviewing job applicants, it's a straightforward book that can help you with your planning. For those applying for jobs, it can be a great "behind the scenes" look at the hiring process. When I read the paragraph urging employers to beware the "professional interviewee," the "candidate who lacks the skills for the job but has developed an understanding of how to manipulate impressions in the interview" (Camp 2001, 70), I had a brief and scary moment of self-realization; I hope I've never manipulated anyone, but anyone who goes to enough interviews does start to develop a sense of what potential employers like to hear. It's nice to know this book is out there advocating effective interviewing techniques, as well as realistically addressing the tricks of the trade.

Gottesman, Deb, and Buzz Mauro, *The Interview Rehearsal Book: 7 Steps to Job-winning Interviews*, New York, Berkley Books, 1999. Deb Gottesman and Buzz Mauro are the directors of Center State Communications, a speech consulting firm that specializes in applying acting skills to speaking and interview. I really like their broadly based approach to interviewing; starting with breathing and relaxation exercises and concluding with an interview dress rehearsal and suggestions for evaluation and follow-up, this is a great book to refer to no matter what kind of job you're interviewing for. They recognize that memorizing typical answers to typical questions is not always the quickest way to a job, and can often cause more stress than it relieves, which I firmly believe as well.

Ream, Richard, "Why Are Manhole Covers Round?" *Information Today*, v. 17, no. 5, May 2000, pps. 26–27. A great short article outlining suggested questions and responses for interviewers and interviewees, as well as suggestions for how the interviewee can best influence the course and flow of an interview. It also includes a sidebar of other sources for question and answer examples.

www.liscareer.com/mckaydunkle_applicants.htm. An excellent article, adapted from Beatrice McKay's and Clare Dunkle's article "Top of the Heap or Bottom of the (Trash) Barrel? Tips for Job Applicants" (in *NMRT Footnotes*, v. 22 n. 2, January 1993). Simple and straightforward, it nonetheless offers a few tips I hadn't thought of previously but agreed with: taking good care of your health beforehand, thanking all of your interviewers immediately, and focusing on your interviewers as people (and taking an interest in them) to lessen your own nervousness.

CHAPTER 8

Interpersonal Communication

Users, some overwhelmed by the swift and radical changes continually taking place in libraries, will be looking toward librarians for those signals that say "May I help you?" instead of "Do not disturb."
 — Marie L. Radford, "Approach or Avoidance? The Role of
 Nonverbal Communication in the Academic Library
 User's Decision to Approach a Reference Librarians"

Technically, interview techniques could have been included in this chapter, which will focus on the challenges and rewards of improving your interpersonal, or one-on-one, communication skills. But first we had to focus on your getting the job. Now we turn our attention to keeping it, which will enable you to teach classes, lead and attend meetings, and speak at conventions (all challenges which will be discussed in the next chapters).

What Are You Saying When You're Not Saying Anything?

Although the opportunities available for librarians to address small groups or even large groups or audiences are becoming more plentiful, the need to speak effectively in interpersonal situations is a need that you will face all day,

every day. Indeed, with the overwhelming preoccupation our profession has with our image, good interpersonal and conversational skills are more important than ever before. Studies have shown that patrons are hesitant to approach us when we appear unapproachable, and the number of articles in the literature about the "us versus them" feeling that often exists between paraprofessionals and librarians is distressingly large. Obviously this is an area in which we could all use a little help, not only in encouraging our patrons to approach us, but also in fostering more open and pleasant work environments.

Reference Service and Other Patron Interactions

The most familiar and common of all interactions with our patrons is the infamous "reference interview." As pointed out by librarian Barbara Conroy, "The communication in an interview is different from that of other face-to-face interactions, in that it focuses on specific information and attempts to eliminate extraneous messages" (Conroy and Jones 1986, 88). Reference interviews vary from job interviews in small but important ways. Job interviews are scheduled whereas reference interviews are not and depend entirely on initiation by the library patron; roles in a job interview are often more clearly defined; and, most often, both parties in a job interview are more highly motivated to interact with each other (the interviewer is eager to fill an open position, and the interviewee is eager to get the job).

Because of those small but significant differences in motivation and the control of initiation, the most important part of the reference interview begins before any verbal communication takes place. Of the utmost importance in working with patrons is being approachable, first, nonverbally and then, verbally. It is not enough to merely station yourself at your library's public service or reference desk. Marie Radford's study of how patrons approach librarians states that the largest group of students, a whopping thirty-eight percent, only ask librarians questions when the librarians initiate the encounter; the next largest number, thirty-five percent, only approached the desk when librarians signaled their availability with eye contact, a smile, or the words "May I help you?" (Radford 1998, 705). If you want more than seventy percent of your patrons to ask you questions, you're clearly going to have to encourage them to. Some ways to do so include the following:

✓ Being aware of all library patrons in your immediate area, at the computer workstations, and in the library at large. Look up and look around: how long has the elementary school child been waiting for an Internet station to open up? How long has someone been looking through your newspaper vertical files? How many CRC handbooks has that undergraduate student retrieved from the reference stacks and flipped through?

✓ Periodically make the physical rounds of your library or work space. Refresh the screens on computer workstations; straighten the books in the stacks; pick up the picture books in the children's area and stack them to be re-shelved. All of these activities are beneficial to the library and your co-workers, and they give patrons a chance to approach you when you are not separated from them by a desk or counter.

✓ Make eye contact with and pleasantly greet as many patrons as possible, either when they pass by your work area or when you pass by them while performing your other work in the library.

✓ Librarian and author Anne J. Mathews recommends these prudent policies: "Ask questions, alternate speaking with listening, and don't engage in other tasks while talking" (Mathews 1983, 9).

Of course working conditions and situations vary so widely in our profession that I offer those tips as the broadest of guidelines for increasing your approachability. The importance of these and other welcoming nonverbal behaviors are well-documented, but until I went to work in a public library I didn't realize how reticent patrons are to "interrupt" librarians who appear busy with other tasks; I am approached with more questions while I am shelving in the stacks, or checking out books at the circulation desk, than I ever receive while staffing the reference desk (illustrating once again the huge need to foster positive and professional service-oriented attitudes at all staff levels). Ironically, it is often the librarians behind the reference desk who must work hardest to encourage patron approach and questions, because they have to overcome the perceived barrier of the reference desk (and computer, and phone...) to establish their approachability.

That is no small challenge. During my first week of work at the public library, I was shocked to learn that all the librarians in our branch worked the reference desk for their entire shift, and that because they had no offices, they had to perform all of their technical, clerical, book selection, and other work requirements while remaining available to answer the phone and patron questions. My prior experience as an academic reference librarian had included, at the most, twenty hours of availability at the reference desk, while the rest of my time was spent in my office, performing my other duties such as webpage maintenance and workshop development. I often left the door open to encourage drop-in questions, but the vast difference in those working environments (just between public and academic, not to mention special and school libraries) was a difficulty to be dealt with. So I do recognize that many librarians often do not mean to appear harried and unapproachable, but are instead in the position of trying to perform detail-oriented and deadline-driven tasks at the same time they are trying to provide public service. On the other hand, all the numbers seem

to indicate that the number of reference questions fielded by reference staff are down, and down significantly; patrons are now as likely as not to turn to the Internet for the ready reference questions that used to be the sole domain of librarians and reference books: "According to the National Center for Education Statistics, reference statistics for all academic libraries fell by almost ten percent from 2.1 million per week in 1994 to 1.9 million per week in 1996 (the latest dates covered)" (Coffman and McGlamery 2000, 66). Students turn to the Internet for research assistance rather than to school and public librarians; undergraduates turn to full-text databases for paper sources rather than to academic librarians and their specialized citation indexes; attorneys and other professionals who used to rely exclusively on their information center staff can now search electronic resources themselves. I do not intend to digress down the well-traveled (and much written about) road claiming that librarians and information professionals are obsolete in the new information economy; rather, I would suggest that we merely need to adjust our roles and skills to address this combination of greater patron access to more and widely varied information sources along with an increasing reticence to ask us questions. One course of action that seems logical is to spend less time answering ready reference questions, and spending more time tutoring and working with patrons more personally, and over a longer period of time. In order to foster that kind of working relationship, and establish a rapport with library users, approachability is an essential first step.

After you have successfully enticed your patrons into actually talking to you, you must turn your attention to what they are saying, as well as to what types of questions you are asking. The types of questions you ask (and the tone in which they are delivered) will determine the types of answers you receive. The most obvious differences between types of questions is the open versus the closed question; for example, if someone asks you where your travel section is, consider these two responses:

> CLOSED: Do you mean travel guide-books? (Can be answered with a yes or no.)
> OPEN: What type of travel resources are you looking for? (Cannot be answered with a yes or no; requires a more specific and informational answer.)

Of course, another option would be to say "over in the 900s," and then return to your cataloging, but this chapter is about improving interpersonal communication, not putting up barriers to it in the form of poor listening and arbitrary answers that may or may not answer the patron's question. Although you will receive very different answers to the questions just listed, closed questions in and of themselves are not inherently inferior to open inquiries; it's the timing that dictates effectiveness. When you get to the stage of confirming whether your patron has found what they need, a yes or no question will be the most expedient way to gauge that. Both open and closed questions serve purposes, and a good rule of thumb is to use open questions to dig for expanded information regarding a person's request, while reserving closed questions to narrow down the informational need or to restate or confirm what you understand to be the request. In pure library-school

jargon, think of open questions as the "or" operator (to expand your search) and closed questions as your "and" operator (to limit your results). For example:

> PATRON: Where's your health section?
> LIBRARIAN: What kind of health information sources are you looking for?
> PATRON: I need to look up some symptoms.
> LIBRARIAN: Do you think this book would help you (displays the Merck manual, open to a page listing diseases and symptoms)?
> PATRON: Yes.

That's vastly simplified, of course (if only all interactions were so immediately successful!), but the point is that a combination of open and closed questions can be used, just like a beautifully ordered search statement ([child or children or kid or kids] and violence and television) to get the information you need to most effectively help your clients.

In the midst of asking questions, you will find yourself once again using the skill encouraged in the first chapter: listening. Engaging in active listening when interacting with your patrons is a vital part of your success in understanding their needs and requests. As is commonly described in library literature, one of the greatest sources of poor communication is "premature diagnosis": a situation wherein the librarian is so eager to make assumptions about the patron's informational needs that he or she jumps to conclusions and attempts to finish the person's questions for them. The easiest way to minimize your chances of developing that habit is to stop trying to immediately paraphrase the request, but rather, listening carefully to it, using pauses afterward to formulate your own thoughts and follow-up questions. That sounds deceptively simple, but yet, we've all sat by people in classes or in meetings who are so eager to speak that they ask questions or make points that were just asked or made (we've all been like that person too; so nervous or eager about speaking that we stop listening in order to gather together the perfect words in our own mind). Having finally started a conversation with a patron, client, or co-workers, the last thing you'll want to do is frustrate them by sending the message that you're not really listening to what they're saying anyway.

The degree of attention you pay to someone is directly related to the success you will have evaluating the nonverbal and verbal feedback cues provided for you during the interaction. As stated by Mathews, "How people relate to, or accept, what the librarian says may have to do with whether they perceive us as understanding them and their interests" (Mathews 1983, 14). Sound familiar? It's all about your audience.

The overall impression I hope to leave you with is that successful interpersonal communication with anyone anywhere (at the reference desk, while training, on the phone) is not something that you can plan and execute in a stereotypically linear fashion. Many communication textbooks, following their "speaker-message-receiver" models, can be misleading in their portrayal of the more informal process. All listening and speaking skills will be utilized at every step of your conversation. Once you have received an answer from an open question, you cannot expect to simply hear it a single time and provide feedback in the form of an instant and perfect answer. You may have to encourage, ask, listen, and rephrase many times in the course of any one interaction. And so, providing positive feedback to a patron who approaches the desk hesitantly may be your first task, in the form of smiling and other verbal and nonverbal cues of encouragement, rather than simply your last, in the form of asking, "Is that the information you were looking for?"

Answering the Phone

Many reference and patron interactions occur via the telephone. It's easy to believe that this is a skill that every librarian should have mastered; many libraries have multiple phone lines and everyone seems, these days, to own a cell phone of their own. However, ask yourself: have you ever been dissatisfied regarding your interaction with someone on the telephone, thanks to their rudeness? Is there anything more frustrating than speaking with someone on the phone who obviously doesn't care about answering your questions, the sole reason you've placed the call?

One of the difficulties of communicating well on the telephone is that the main parties can't see each other; I've had to explain to my niece many times that the person on the other end cannot see that she's smiling, or pointing, or nodding. We need to remind not only four-year-olds but ourselves as well that we must therefore put more emphasis on developing our vocabularies and, just as important, our voices, our tone. For those of us who have heard our own voices on a recording and are less than impressed with them, take heart. And it is cliché, but I assure you that patrons can hear it when you smile over the telephone. In fact, smiling cannot only be heard, but it may also be an important part of helping yourself feel more cheerful. At least one psychological research study has found that voluntarily smiling can actually produce a positive change in emotion; "Our results suggest it may be possible for an individual to choose when to generate some of the physiological changes that occur during a spontaneous emotion — by simply making a facial expression" (Ekman and Davidson 1993, 345).

A large number of the strategies in this book are to encourage you to remove your own mental barriers before approaching the speaking process, and eliminating possible problems before they develop. You may be busy, the phone may be ringing constantly, and you may feel rushed, but it doesn't take any longer to answer the phone cheerfully than it does begrudgingly. I'll be the first to admit I've had bad days at the reference desk (who hasn't?) and have been guilty of answering the phone with a "don't bother me now" tone. Trust me, it causes pauses and stuttering, followed by righteous anger, on the other end of the line; patrons can hear the true message behind your words.

Thankfully, righting the situation is not complicated. All that's necessary for a successful phone conversation is for you to do the following:

✓ Answer the phone quickly and cheerfully.

✓ Identify your library or yourself (not everyone is comfortable providing a first name, nor is it necessary; a simple "Springfield Public Library, how can I help you?" will always suffice).

✓ Verbally verify the caller's request and provide verbal encouragement such as "So you're asking for..." or "what you're looking for is..." or even "uh-huh, go on..."

✓ If you can provide an answer quickly, do so, and don't be afraid to let your caller know what you're up to ("I think I can find that, I'm just going to do a quick search on the catalog right now...").

✓ If it's a longer question or you may have to refer it to someone else or consult with your colleagues, always give the caller options; ask if they would prefer to wait on hold or receive a return call or e-mail as soon as you have the answer.

If a person is ringing with a comment or concern, rather than a question, lend a sympathetic ear, be friendly, and if you are the appropriate person for them to address, do your best to answer their concern or provide a plan for future interaction or conflict resolution. If you are not the staff person who can best resolve a caller's issue (for example, a technical services person may wish to refer a parent's concern about a children's book the library owns to the Youth Services librarian), listen carefully until you can appropriately direct the call or assure the patron that they will receive a call from the professional in the best position to help. Above all, in these situations, endeavor to keep your tone and language positive; if callers perceive that you are dismissing them out of hand or interrupting their discourse to pass them on, any conversation will slowly but surely deteriorate into an unpleasant situation, and no one wants that. At the same time, it is not anyone's job to accept verbal abuse or to completely disregard or change policies or procedures to satisfy any one patron's suggestion. The overall goal is one of pleasant moderation, which can be achieved through a variety of phrases, a few of which are: I can understand why you find this frustrating; would you like to speak with our director about it? Perhaps she could better answer all of your questions. Our children's librarian is in today and is more familiar with that book; would you like to speak with him about it? Thank you for the purchase recommendation; I'm sorry we don't have the book you need. We can certainly try to get it for you through interlibrary loan. Would you have any interest in that?

Useful phrases that can be used to bridge what the patron is saying to our questions and replies are called transition phrases. Transition phrases like "I appreciate that, but..." or "I respect what you're saying, but..." can also help buy you some time before replying; they can also "nicely give you permission to control the conversation, and to say what needs to be said" (Goodman 2000, 48) Last but not least, always remember that "Listening is particularly important to those who rely on the telephone to communicate with customers because there are no visual clues to affirm or negate information" (Powerful Telephone Skills 1993, 48).

Training

Staff training and professional development techniques are quite widely available in the library literature, but I believe the topic merits inclusion here as the first matter through which staff learn to interact with one another. A good training experience for both trainer and trainee can lead to improved communication and relations throughout the workplace, which is beneficial to both staff and patrons.

The first requirement is to implement a training program; a 1995 ACRL (Association of College and Research Libraries) study reported that forty-two percent of college libraries had a training program for their newly hired reference librarians, yet only eight percent of the same libraries had written policies or goal statements for whatever training programs they had (Robles and Wyatt 1996, 4). In the detail-oriented and diverse work situations in which librarians and other library staff routinely perform their duties, a solid and quantitative knowledge base, instilled through comprehensive training, is imperative. Nothing says "welcome" to a new employee or "keep up the good work" to a current employee like enjoyable and efficient staff training programs can; conversely, nothing indicates a lack of interest in promoting a new hire's sense of belonging more than a lackluster or poorly organized training program or opportunities. Good training is not complicated to provide but it does depend on the trainer's willingness to provide it, as well as that trainer's desire to further their own speaking and communication skills by learning about, planning, and implementing a cohesive system.

Be aware of the training environment, and have a plan. Research shows that it is important to encourage conditions that positively influence the relationship between the teacher and the learner, conditions that include "the level of participation, respect, collaboration, reflection and practice, and empowerment" (Jurow 2001, 7). Though you will not have to expend energy enticing someone you're training to approach you (chances are they're scheduled to train with you or have an allotted time period with you in which to learn what you're there to teach), don't abandon entirely the skills learned to encourage patrons to feel comfortable around you; anyone's early days at a new job are often extremely stressful and prone to information overload, and as a trainer, you must always indicate, verbally and nonverbally, your willingness to answer any questions and concerns. That means pausing frequently to ask if your trainee has any questions; restating their questions to make sure you're appropriately answering them; developing your own personal style to make the experience entertaining and interesting; and above all, developing and following a strategic plan for the session.

Much as agendas provide the framework and goals for meetings, a formal or informal written training plan can provide both trainer and trainee with training structure and achievable objectives. I have had many first days, both in professional and paraprofessional (as well as student) library positions, and the only consistent characteristic among all of them was either poorly organized or nonexistent training; I experienced the most glaring example at my very first library job, in which I was expected to supervise and close the entire library on what was only my second five-hour shift there. Instead of learning the basic components of my new job, all I remember doing that night was hoping that there wouldn't be a fire drill or any other building emergency. Therefore, I advise you to make an agenda or outline for yourself and for the person you are training; it will help remind you which topics to cover, and it will provide your

trainee with a broad overview of what they will be learning. Most importantly, it can help you make sure the topics are appropriate for a new hire, and are provided in the most helpful order. In many ways, preparing such an agenda will be just like making the broad outline for a presentation; write down your main objectives and what you know about them, do a little supplementary research or fine-tuning of information so you can be ready for any questions; and then organize them logically.

Be approachable and share resources. In addition to being cognizant of any new co-worker's first-day discomfiture, you will want to strive to provide the most open learning environment possible. That means an upbeat tone of voice, positive reinforcement in the form of frequent smiles and gentle reminders or encouragement, and above all, a display of enthusiasm for your training task, as well as your trainee's job. No one likes to be trained by someone who is only doing so begrudgingly or because it's "part of the job description." That kind of attitude is easily discerned and can lead to discomfort and reticence to ask necessary questions on the part of the trainee. Even if training, like public speaking, is not something you do often or feel that you do really well, try to view it as a challenge, or as a way to distinguish yourself in the workplace, and maintain a positive outlook. Having a plan also means having the appropriate resources available to share with the person you are training; make sure that you have all of the procedure manuals, keyboard shortcut cheat sheets, policy statements, and any other tools you may need to sufficiently train the person. Having to constantly interrupt a training, meeting, or instruction session to run and make extra copies of certain documents is frustrating for and insulting to your participants, and it reflects poorly on your ability to plan ahead and organize a cohesive presentation.

Ask questions and record achievements. Just as the shortest distance between two points is a straight line, the quickest way to find out what someone is learning is to ask them. If you've done what you could to make the training well-structured and enthusiastic, you needn't worry that you will be putting your new or continuing co-worker "on the spot." After covering a topic or procedure, simply ask a few open questions to determine if the person is learning what you've been teaching, and always finish up by asking them, sincerely, the most important question of all: "Do you have any questions for me?" If you have scheduled short breaks or hands-on practice sessions (always a good idea, by the way, with or without guided exercises to gain proficiency), a good time to ask that is after the break or practice session. That way the trainee is not fixated on the upcoming break, or may have thought of questions during their hands-on learning; asking then also indicates that you're more willing to answer any questions than to simply plow ahead and "get through" the rest of the training.

Sometimes you have to ask more direct questions of audiences who are not participating or interacting with you, and you may have to be more blunt in your approach with a person who never has any questions. There is always the chance that they understand you and the task perfectly, but there's also a chance that they are not focused enough on the training, or are reticent for other reasons, to ask questions. In those situations you may have to more carefully

question the person on the task at hand, for example: "If I asked you for a print-out of everything I have checked out, how would you do that?" As you will learn later, that is also an important way to collect feedback and tailor your training to your trainee. If all of your questions are being satisfactorily answered, you may have to view that as a cue that your training pace is too slow, or that you are not covering enough information to keep your trainee challenged. Ask questions, listen carefully to the answers, and adjust your interaction accordingly.

Recording achievements is more important symbolically. Unlike asking questions, which you should be doing to encourage interaction and gather feedback, recording achievements or checking off training items completed is a more tangible way to indicate to both training parties that progress is indeed being made. Who doesn't enjoy crossing things off the to-do list? It also helps you keep track of where you are in the training process, in case you are not the only one doing the staff training, or the training will extend over a period of several sessions or days. If you have created an agenda or training outline, use it to mark when objectives are fulfilled, as well as to take notes on questions your trainee asks, or suggestions of your own for further refinements or additions to your training plan.

Evaluate feedback and remain accessible. Teaching another person is a very specialized form of interpersonal communication, and as such, it is vital that you remain open to noticing and analyzing feedback during the training session. Like smaller or more informal library instruction sessions, training gives you the unique opportunity to personally adapt your presentation to your receiver. It also gives you the chance to view your tasks and professional duties from a different point of view; in remaining open to questions and encouraging your trainee to perform tasks in a hands-on fashion, you may learn something new yourself. Although you will eventually hone your own training style, you must also be flexible and alter it when necessary. If you are dealing with a person whom you can tell is very nervous about operating the keyboard or other equipment while you watch, you may wish to alternate duties with the person, perhaps offering to type while he or she tells you the commands; you could also provide them with a guided practice worksheet and let them work through it alone for a few moments. Just as all trainers are different, so are all trainees; one month you may work side by side with a new hire at the reference desk, answering questions simultaneously and taking turns functioning as the other's shadow; the next month you may train someone who is obviously uncomfortable answering questions in tandem but is much more at ease working the desk alone, but with you available as a backup.

Although it is important to check off objectives as they are attained, it is also important to view training for what it is: a never-ending process. If you have ever been trained by someone who obviously couldn't wait to be done with it, you know how distracting and distressing that is, in no small part because it makes you want to be done with learning and asking questions for good, too. It is much better to assure anyone you've trained that you fully expect to continue answering any questions that might occur to them as the job unfolds, and that you look forward to working with

them in all ways possible. That should be second nature; if you didn't want to answer questions, why did you become a librarian? Besides, a little bit of accessibility goes a long way. If the people you have trained feel comfortable turning to you in the future with questions or requests for assistance, you have increased your chances of developing a sure and able staff, one that creates fewer problems out of ignorance and fear, and that will make the workplace a better place for everyone.

If you do any reading or research on communication theories and techniques, you may also want to spend some time learning about instructional design, which can help you develop and organize your library's training programs. Instructional design involves a number of tasks, but its learning curve is no higher than that of learning to facilitate group discussions; its basic principles include "analyzing your needs, describing tasks, writing objectives, developing tests, formulating instructional strategies, developing materials, and preparing evaluations" (Weaver-Meyers 2001, 126).

Playing Nice with Everyone

Any chapter in a book for librarians that discusses interpersonal communication would be remiss if it didn't address the rift in the profession between professional and paraprofessional staff members. Entire research works have been produced on the subject (*The Library Paraprofessional: Notes from the Underground*, by Terry Rodgers, McFarland & Company, 1997, is one very fine example) and numerous studies have been carried out by former paraprofessional Larry R. Oberg and other scholars in the field. Oberg said it best when he asserted that "anecdotal evidence indicates that librarians and paraprofessionals often misunderstand each others' roles ... as early as 1977, Richard M. Dougherty pointed to a growing rift in the relations between professionals and other library staff" (Oberg 1992, 103). With more paraprofessionals than ever staffing reference desks and performing ever more tasks that used to be the sole province of librarians, as well as the appearance of many other specialized library personnel who are not technically librarians (information technology staff people, or human resources and library funding specialists, for example), it's important to realize that a large part of being a true "professional" is treating others as such, regardless of their job titles or seniority.

As a public library paraprofessional (my current title is that of Library Assistant, a position for which a master's of library science degree is still required), I have my own anecdotal evidence that indicated the importance of this subject to me. While staffing the reference desk with one of our branch's librarians, a woman approached and asked which one of us was the librarian. Because I was the one she addressed and because my colleague was engaged in printing out handouts for her book talk, I replied, "Either one of us.... What is your question?" As the patron began to speak, the librarian looked up from the printer and interjected, "Actually, that depends on the question," at which point the patron addressed the question to her. The communication miscues in this situation are obvious; I might have responded to the patron in a way that indicated we were both available to answer her question, but that my colleague was the librarian; the librarian, meanwhile, could have

monitored the situation and involved herself in the interaction in a way that I wouldn't have perceived as a disparagement of my ability.

Libraries, as an institution, have traditionally been perceived as one of the great arbiters of democracy. It would be a misfortune to endanger that reputation by indicating to our patrons and those in other professions that we can't all work harmoniously with one another for the greater good. We've come a long way since Larry Oberg (a paraprofessional at the time) and his future wife (a librarian) had to stage a sit-in to be allowed to sit together in their library's break room (Oberg 1993, 8), but we've still got a long way to go.

Chapter Summary

Good public speaking skills can also be applied to interpersonal communication settings, such as interactions with library patrons, in particular, the reference interview and phone conversations. The most important part of the reference interview is getting patrons to approach and ask you questions, a feat that can be achieved through a number of verbal and nonverbal techniques such as initiating the contact, making yourself available by walking through the library and workspace, making eye contact with and smiling at patrons, and then asking them if you can be of assistance. After contact has been made, listening and speaking skills both must be utilized to understand the patron's information request, and open and closed questions must be asked in order to continue or to assess the interaction.

Interacting with patrons on the telephone is another aspect of providing reference and patron service that can be enhanced by improving all of your speaking skills. Answer the phone promptly and with a pleasant tone of voice (no matter what you're doing or how you feel), identify yourself or your institution, listen sympathetically to your caller and make an effort to connect them with the most appropriate staff person to consider their question or concern, give the caller options ("Would you like to continue to hold, or shall I give you a call back in a few moments?"), and make use of transition phrases to show empathy and gain time to formulate the proper response.

Improving your interpersonal communication skills will not only help you better understand and relate to your patrons, it will also make you a better trainer and colleague. The most important part of training another person is having a comprehensive and organized plan for doing so; analyze your training objectives and the best ways to achieve those objectives, and don't forget to devise a method to evaluate the results of the training for both trainer and trainee. Be approachable and share resources with your trainees and other employees, ask questions to periodically gauge your trainee's interest and understanding of the subject matter, and carefully record or recognize achievements and completed objectives.

In a profession like librarianship, which employs a diverse range of people who often differ in their attitudes and experiences, it is important to treat all co-workers with the respect that you yourself expect. In creating a work environment where there is little or no tension between you and your colleagues, you'll be creating a library environment that your patrons (and visiting library administrators) will perceive as collegial and conducive to their own study, work, and recreation (as well as deserving of their support, budgetary and otherwise).

Further Reading

Avery, Elizabeth Fuseler, Terry Dahlin, and Deborah A. Carver, eds. 2001. *Staff Development: A Practical Guide*. 3rd ed. Chicago and London: American Library Association. Of particular interest in this comprehensive guide for keeping your staff well trained and happy is Susan Jurow's chapter entitled "How People Learn: Applying Adult Learning Theory and Learning Styles Models to Training Sessions." The entire book is a great look at how to specifically create and tailor training sessions for and to your entire staff.

Fatt, James P.T. 1999. It's Not What You Say, It's How You Say It. *Communication World* 16 (6):37–40. If you want a better understanding of what you're saying even when you're not saying anything, read this article to learn about five main categories of nonverbal communication: eye contact, gestures, posture, paralanguage, and overall facial expression. Your audience will determine your credibility and competence based on more on those characteristics than on your actual words.

Goodman, Gary S. 2000. *Please Don't Shoot the Messenger: How to Talk to Demanding Bosses, Clueless Colleagues, Tough Customers, and Difficult Clients Without Losing Your Cool (Or Your Job!)*. Chicago, Illinois: Contemporary Books. This one's a little heavy on the true customer service (as applies to retail and business) approach, but Chapter 8, entitled "How To Prevent Communication Mishaps and Miscues," succinctly lists ways to effectively interact with both customers (patrons) and your co-workers.

Zahn, David. 1998. Lessons from the Front, Back, and Sides of the Room. *Training & Development* 52 (1):12–13. A short but helpful article outlining what can and does go wrong during most training sessions, and how you can avoid most problems en route to facilitating your own sessions.

http://www.ssdesign.com/librarypr/index.html. The Library Marketing and PR website offers a variety of helpful articles and tools (including free clip art and fonts) to help you get the word out regarding your great library. This site promises (and delivers) "Strategies, Techniques, Resources, Tips, and Tools for Library Communicators."

CHAPTER 9

Library Instruction

The way to learn the art of teaching is by imitation. To teach well one should have had at least one good teacher and been struck, consciously or not, by the means employed and the behavior displayed.
— Jacques Barzun, *Begin Here*

When I was an academic librarian, I had a love-hate relationship with the entire concept of bibliographic instruction. I worked in an engineering and science library, and I loved teaching workshops and introductory sessions to the engineering students, particularly the undergraduates. They were very smart, and often funny, and their desire to jump through the required hoop of library instruction without paying too much attention to it could often be quite endearing. Trust me, you haven't seen cute until you've been pitied by an eighteen-year-old engineer-to-be who can't imagine why he would ever need the library in this age of the Internet. Mostly they're cute because you know the next time you see them they'll need your help finding those older government documents on microfiche, but that's another subject.

What is not cute, or at least wasn't for me, was the endless amount of conferences, roundtable discussions, e-mails, listservs, and general meeting time that surrounded the process of teaching library skills (or, as it's commonly re-

ferred to now, "information literacy"). In any given semester I might have spent up to forty hours, total, preparing and giving workshops and sessions, but I can promise you that every semester I spent at least twice that amount of time going to campus meetings and committee roundtables about those workshops and our teaching methodologies. That is not to say that some discussion and reflection on different teaching tips and speaking tricks among professionals is a bad thing, but the deliberation did seem disproportionate to the amount of face time we actually had with students.

Putting Our Money Where Our Mouths Are

Teaching librarians at the university where I worked were not considered faculty, or tenure track, but we were inundated with meetings and retreats to improve our teaching skills. The more such meetings I was required to attend, the more frustrated I became. The meetings invariably showed all the signs of a general lack of public speaking skills: they were often disorganized, there was never any clear agenda, the speakers were dispassionate, and nobody ever left until consensus had been reached on the perfect "script" or "format" or "method," or, at the most useless, until everyone had agreed that blue paper was the best color on which to photocopy our library handout (a discussion that clocked in at just under an hour, if I remember correctly). The saddest fact was that in all of this discussion regarding examples and handout colors, nobody ever addressed the basic fundamentals of teaching: getting a class's attention, keeping it, and fostering discussion with your students.

Library instruction combines the skills of public speaking with those of teaching. Like teaching, it has its own set of occupational fears (which are often added to the broader fear of public speaking a librarian may already be susceptible to). Marilyn Lutzker sums up the dangers nicely in her chapter in the book *Teaching Librarians to Teach.* According to Lutzker, "Fear of not being able to answer questions, fear of not being able to think fast enough, fear of embarrassment, fear of the unknown and unexpected, fear of not being in control" are the fears that make many librarians react negatively to the idea of teaching (Lutzker 1986, 14). Providing library instruction means engaging in small group communication, which differs from the stereotypical public speaking (large group) environment in several important and challenging ways. Thorough research and preparation is more important than ever; the format should encourage active learning (as opposed to passive listening, which is more common in large lecture groups); ex-temporaneous speaking (speaking from an outline or notes) really is the easiest and most effective format for instruction; and your availability and ability to answer audience questions can be even more important than your prepared statements.

Research and Preparation

It is a given that you should always prepare for any kind of talk carefully, because in any situation there is the chance that you will be asked to answer questions. That chance, in library instruction, becomes a certainty. When you are teaching students or fellow colleagues how to use a database, it is not enough for you to know only the way you prefer to search it. You must learn every way to use that product, including search methods you would never use, or using those functions and tricks that you think are too specific to be of much practical use. Every person has a different learning style and will search for information differently. It is up to you, as the teacher, to at least be familiar with as many aspects of the subject or database you're teaching as you can. That is not to say that any workshop you give has to be a jumble of every possible manner of searching a database; that would be terrible. It simply means that you must be aware of different ways to obtain the same information, so that during the hands-on period of the workshop, you can show the person who is struggling to find results different ways of obtaining them.

Although it can sometimes be a challenge to get questions started in small instruction sessions, there is also a danger from the other side of the spectrum to consider. Often you will encounter attendees who are there primarily to show off their knowledge by questioning yours. A typical such encounter might run something like this:

> LIBRARIAN: Let's start by searching the catalog for a specific title.
>
> STUDENT: (Waving hand wildly) My undergraduate thesis is in the library here; do you have an example or could we search for that?
>
> LIBRARIAN: I do have an example, but let's try your title just for fun.
>
> STUDENT: (After the class searches for the title) How can you find dissertations that your library doesn't own?
>
> LIBRARIAN: Well, for that we search a database called Dissertations Abstracts, but that's not a topic we can tackle today; you're welcome to stay after the workshop and I can speak about it with you. Now, moving on to searching for authors....

I'm not saying that happens often, but it does happen. The important thing to remember is that the cardinal rule of instruction sessions, like meetings, is not to get unnecessarily sidetracked. Be polite, be interested, be as helpful as you can be within your time constraints, but be firm: you are the person teaching, and it is your responsibility to ensure that all participants walk away having learned what you set out to teach.

In addition to requiring more and very careful research and an inside-and-out knowledge of your subject, preparing for your instruction session means more time spent on setting realistic goals and organizing your material to fit

within your allotted time. Many novice bibliographic instruction librarians struggle with combining their perceived need to cover everything and the realistic time and attention limits of the class. When dealing with students, from high school to college and beyond, no goal is too small or too insignificant to be listed and considered time-consuming. You must be pragmatic when determining goals; if you're facing a group of first-year college students for whom learning library skills is low on the list of the day's priorities, teaching them that you, as a librarian or professional, are friendly, approachable, and knowledgeable is an accomplishment. List it and consider ways to achieve it.

> GOAL ONE: Show that librarians are here to help.
>
> TO ACHIEVE: Arrive at class early, meet students at door with handouts.
>
> Somewhere in introduction, state reference desk hours and e-mail and refer to them on handout.
>
> Ask for questions after each main point and during conclusion.
>
> Allow fifteen minutes for self-directed student practice.
>
> Have three research questions ready for not-so-self-directed students.

All of your objectives should be broken down to their most basic components, and you should be prepared with several different approaches to achieve all of them. Simply stating that you want your students to learn the "best possible way to search Nexis/Lexis" is not going to get the job done, though it will make you more nervous, because it is unrealistic. A quick listing of possible components that could come under that broad goal should indicate the enormity of it, which, as someone who uses it daily, you might be forgetting:

Obtaining access to Nexis, in the library and at home.

Choosing the most appropriate library to search for your needs.

Searching Nexis by keyword.

Searching Nexis by date.

Searching Nexis by publication name.

Searching Nexis by subject.

Limiting your results by keyword, date, publication name, subject, etc.

Saving your search results.

E-mailing your search results.

Printing your search results.

Determining the value of your search results.

Citation information provided by Nexis.

Text/Image availability in Nexis.

Dates of inclusion and coverage of Nexis.

That list took me about two minutes to compile, and should give you a real appreciation for the true measure of your task. By doing this work ahead of time, rather than when you're facing a group of a people, you should drastically reduce your fears that you will be unable to fill the class time or adequately answer questions.

When planning a workshop in conjunction with a teacher or professor who wants to bring a group of people to you (either attending a session at the library or inviting you to come and speak with the class), another important aspect of preparing is to communicate as effectively as possible with that coordinator. Ask questions regarding what the students have been learning, how many of them there are, and most importantly, what their professor or teacher wants you to achieve during your session. That will help you more effectively suit your presentation to the class's needs. If the instructor wants you to cover the basics of using the library in general, you will need to prepare quite a different set of goals and outlines than if the teacher tells you his or her students are currently writing research papers on assigned topics and need to know how to use a general periodicals database. You may not see them as often but these coordinators are every bit as much your colleagues as the people you work with daily and share an office with, and it is important for you to foster a good working relationship with them if you are going to be an effective instructor of their classes.

Encouraging Active Learning

Traditional public speaking handbooks rarely address how to interact with your audience if you are trying to teach them something. They may tell you how to inform an audience, or how to persuade an audience, but if you're looking for true instructional techniques, it is often more useful to turn to educators or education theorists. Your desired outcome in a library workshop or class is not only to engage your audience, but to motivate them as well: "The ideal lesson begins with motivating the learner; for example, tell students what they will get out of the class, even if it is just a faster way to do their homework" (Barclay 1995, 25). At the same time, you must speak effectively enough to achieve a set of specific objectives and to engage your listeners in the active learning process.

That does not mean that your class will be a failure if you can't hold it in a state-of-the-art computer lab and provide hands-on library skills practice, or even if you can't hold it in the library at all. It does mean that you must not only get the audience's interest with a solid introduction, but you must also encourage questions, discussion, and interaction throughout your lesson plan. Small workshops and classes can provide you with a wonderful opportunity to interact with your patrons or co-workers on a more informal basis. Although it is never a good idea to completely eschew formality and you must always be courteous and professional, speaking with three to five people, or even as many as twenty, in a classroom or lab setting provides an opportunity to try out some of your more outrageous and fun attention-getters and introductory tactics.

You should also remain more open to customizing your session "on the fly" to respond to the needs of your audience, which can be accomplished by carefully monitoring the feedback you receive while talking with them. Customizing, however, is not the same as digressing; if your main objectives for an introductory Internet session are to explain the concept of browsers, teach basic navigation skills, and introduce the users to a reputable search engine, it stands to reason that somewhere *within* those broadly based guidelines, you will be able to incorporate suggestions from your audience. One mode of doing so is to ask your patrons what terms they would like to search the Internet for; they will remember your session much better if they're searching for things they're in-

terested for, rather than being forced to go into yahoo.com and enter the search "knitting+patterns+quilts." That may be your favorite topic and the best search statement you've found, but you'll be missing the point: you already know how to search the Internet. Your patrons, if they signed up for an introductory session, don't. So step back and let them search it.

Too many librarians make the mistake of assuming that each search they demonstrate (on the Internet, in databases, in the library catalog) must be the "perfect example." Not only is that hard work for the librarian (who must find the perfect search, memorize it, and then hope that the results stay exactly the same from day to day), it's unrealistic and dull for your audience. How many times have you, a trained professional who most likely spent some time with Venn diagrams in library school, chanced upon the "perfect search" on your first try? Trust your audience enough to allow them to experiment during your workshop as they would in a real life situation, when you won't be standing right there with them. More often than not, I've seen audience-driven presentations yield more interesting searches and pitfalls to discuss, and also better results. I've also seen librarians self-destruct when a search they performed the day before their workshop retrieved slightly different results than the search performed during the presentation (with constantly growing and changing databases, that is only to be expected), losing their place and feeling like failures because the wonderful example changed. The key is to strike a balance between being well-prepared and remaining open to spontaneity and audience participation. It's a balance that becomes easier and more fun to strike every time you present a workshop, I promise.

Speaking Extemporaneously

Webster's defines *extemporaneous* as "composed, performed, or uttered on the spur of the moment; carefully prepared but delivered without notes or text." Most public speaking textbooks place extemporaneous speaking between impromptu (completely made up on the spot) and reading from a prepared manuscript; Stephen Lucas states that "most experienced speakers prefer the extemporaneous method, and most teachers emphasize it" (Lucas 1998, 270). Thank you, Professor Lucas, and exactly where were you when I suffered through countless bibliographic instruction committee meetings with librarians convinced they had to have a word-by-word script to read from before they dared face a class?

I would like to go on record here: You do not need a script to be an effective teacher or speaker. You do not need the perfect example to illustrate your point. You do not need to use the exact same words as your colleagues are using, or repeat yourself exactly to every class to be a valuable part of your institution's greater plan for instilling information literacy skills. Some consistency and agreement between co-workers and colleagues is necessary to ensure that across a campus or other setting, students are receiving the best possible skills and workshops that we, as librarians, can provide. Can you imagine the indignation (or laughter) you'd face, however, if you dared suggest that all the English or history professors at your school read from the same consensus-created "script," or that they all use the exact same example with all of their classes? That wouldn't fly for a second, and as teachers and professionals ourselves, we shouldn't accept it either. Acknowledge that common goals and expectations are necessary, and if it is required that you follow a prepared script that someone else has written, look upon it more as a guideline for preparing your own extemporaneous presentation.

Speaking extemporaneously allows you the freedom of moving your presentation along at your audience's pace, as well as giving you more chances to tailor your talk to your students. Bibliographic instruction gives us the truly wonderful opportunity to actually go right to the students and ask them for their questions and opinions, as opposed to our usually passive duty of staffing the reference desk until they decide to come up to us and ask their questions. Here's an opportunity we shouldn't waste. Of course, this chance for interaction with the audience is what tends to make many librarians and inexperienced teachers nervous; there are very few surprises involved when you simply read a script and an example verbatim from your notes. Wilbert J. McKeachie offers a number of very helpful tips for encouraging questioning and discussion in your library instruction sessions, including the following.

✓ Invite your students to write down their answers to your questions, calling on them only after they've written down something that they can read aloud when called upon. That helps them to feel less nervous about forgetting the words they want to use.

✓ Invite the class to discuss your question or suggestion with the person next to them, or invite them to work in small groups, and then elicit responses from them as pairs. That helps diffuse the responsibility among the partners, but you must be careful to circulate among the class and make sure everyone is communicating with his or her partner. I won't lie to you; depending on the class, monitoring an exercise like that may feel more like mediating interpersonal disputes on a grade-school playground, but for the most part, students are remarkably good about working with whomever they're near, especially if it's only for a short time during the class period.

✓ Use generalized questions to ensure that a wide variety of answers will be "right" ones, and be appreciative and encouraging of the students who respond to your queries (McKeachie 1999, 55–56).

By asking for input and suggestions from your class, you will not only make your presentation much more pertinent and useful for them, you'll make it more interesting for yourself. Imagine if I had asked my engineering students to search the periodicals databases for articles on "violence and children and television," which was the scripted example that all undergraduate students were supposed to search during the workshop. Had I used that example, those science students would probably have been very uninterested in the subject matter, in addition to gaining experience in searching humanities databases, which, after the workshop, they probably never would have used or seen again. By asking each class what subjects they were currently studying, however, the teachers would be able to help them do searches on such topics as fuel and electricity hybrid engines, ethical issues in bioengineering, and the production output of various factory and manufacturing plant layout designs, all in engineering and science databases that they might have some use for in the future.

One last difficulty that following a written script can cause is the lack of good and necessary redundancy (see chapter 3). If you are presenting users with completely new information and definitions, or doing a demonstration that is very detailed, you will need to repeat yourself, during the course of your talk: "Although readers can look back to such information when needed, listeners cannot stop the current flow of information and 'play back' previous utterances ... therefore it is useful to repeat certain information in somewhat different ways during the course of a lecture" (Day 1980, 98). You may feel that it is harder to speak from notes or an outline, but any slight repetitions those notes cause you to make may actually help your listeners.

Answering Questions Any Time, All the Time

Librarians and information professionals spend most of their work lives hoping their patrons will overcome their hesitancy to "interrupt" or "be a bother" and approach them with their questions and research needs. Providing library instruction, as I stated earlier, gives us the rare chance to go to them. Instruction does not need to end when your one allotted fifty-minute classroom session does; include your library's business card or contact information with any handouts you send with your students. If you offer services such as live or e-mail reference assistance, journal article delivery services, or one-on-one research appointments, make sure to mention them to the students. After the class is over, invite anyone with additional questions to speak to you, and then stay in the classroom or other setting until every one of them has left. You won't get many takers, but that is the nature of any advertising and promotion (just ask people who compile and collect surveys for a living about their response rate). Be patient, be available, and be generous with your contact information and services, and use your workshop time to increase your visibility within your organization's structure (regardless of whether your organization is a college, a business, a school, or a public library).

Sending something with your audience is also a valuable way to remind them that you are there solely to assist them and to provide (for the most part, completely free of charge) patron or customer service. If you're teaching an Internet workshop, compile a short list of search engine URLs that you like to use (I myself am eternally grateful to the academic librarian who cited the search engine ixquick.com on a handout she gave me; I use it every day, and everyone I show it to has never heard of it before!). If you're teaching other staff members how to use PowerPoint, create a small list of common keystroke shortcuts that you use; if you're giving a book or informative talk to a group that is meeting in your library, provide a short list of suggested reading, or an outline of your talk and suggestions for further research. When I staff the reference desk, I always notice that nothing makes people happier than a free printout of an article, or a photocopy from a reference book or other resource that they can take with them. There may be no such thing as a free lunch, but there is such a thing as free workshops, which can be supplemented with free information and tips.

Teaching Isn't Confined to the Classroom: Book Talks and Tours

Book Talks

Is the printed word dead? Sadly, the point is actually debated, and provides the subject matter for many articles and books. We won't address the question here, but will merely assume that the printed word has not been beaten yet, and as such, it will remain the responsibility of library professionals to give inspiring and useful book talks. Book talks are a slightly different animal from the types of public speaking we've discussed thus far. They are really an opportunity to not only talk about books and reading, but to sell books and reading. As such, they must be approached from a more sales-oriented point of view.

For a brief period after college, my brother worked as a door-to-door insurance salesman. He still relates tales of early-morning sessions where the entire sales staff had to stand up, get moving, and cheer along with such mottoes as "How's your P.M.A.?" (P.M.A. stood for "positive mental attitude.") And the horror stories of Wal-Mart employees being forced to start their work shifts with pro-company cheers and rallies are well-documented. Thankfully, most of us don't have to sell insurance or merchandise, so I'm not suggesting that you and your colleagues get together and have library pep rallies. I am suggesting, however, that you have to recognize that sales professionals do take getting themselves "fired up" very seriously — and so should you, however you have to accomplish it.

The basics of good book talking are simple and adhere closely to the more general principles of good public speaking. Know your audience, and try to predict what kind of books and resources they will find most interesting and useful. Within those parameters, pick books and other sources that you are familiar with, and most importantly, that you are excited about or at least have some kind of strong feelings about. Be well prepared, by having a number of the books you'll be talking about along with you, as well as making sure that extra copies can be found in your institution to supply the demand you hope to create. Focus on having a conversation with your audience about the materials you've chosen, rather than hiding behind a prepared written or memorized speech; your listeners will be busy thinking about the book you're holding up, not whether you're picking the best words or most eloquent sentences to summarize and review them.

Although I firmly believe that you must find your own style for presenting, and it must be in a manner that makes you comfortable speaking to an audience, I have to say that I think speaking extemporaneously is the easiest way to give book talks. Extemporaneous speaking allows you to be flexible, and the ability to be flexible is priceless, especially when giving book talks, which are typically informal in structure. When I gave a talk on agricultural fiction, nonfiction, and video resources to a group of senior citizens, it turned out that the vast majority of them had already watched one of my video selections, "The Farmer's Wife," when it aired on public television. Although I had planned to outline the story and setting of the three-video set, once I learned that almost everyone had seen it and already knew the plot, I was able to skip that synopsis and focus on my next resource, a novel by Wendell Berry, instead. In contrast to "The Farmer's Wife," hardly any of my audience members knew who Wendell Berry was, and those who did know of him had been unaware that in addition to being a prominent essayist and poet, Berry was also a novelist. Because I had spent less time on the video information, which the audience didn't really need, we were able to much more deeply discuss Berry's other novels and works. My written outline, placed discreetly on the table at my side where the books and videotapes were placed, had included lengthier notes on "The Farmer's Wife," but no one in the audience knew (or would have cared even if they did) that I'd skipped most of it, just as I'd added things about Wendell Berry that were nowhere to be found in my outline. If I'd taken the time and trouble to write my book talk out word for word, I might have felt so invested in it that I had to read it verbatim, which would have bored my audience.

Constantly remind yourself that trying to achieve some impossible standard of "remembering everything" or "saying everything perfectly" is not only unattainable, but your audience wouldn't know even if you did perform a miracle and say everything you wanted to, using the perfect words to do so. So why make that your goal? I saw evidence of this desire for perfection just last week when I attended a Pampered Chef party, where a friend of mine gave a demonstration of how to make vegetable pizza while using a variety of Pampered Chef kitchen tools. It was her first such presentation, and we all felt she did a great job. She showed us several different tools, gave us cooking tips, and made a delicious pizza for us. When we told her afterward how well she'd done, she thanked us while flipping frantically through her note cards and bemoaning the many things she'd forgotten to tell us. Her apology was unnecessary, and had this been a professional situation, it would have been a mistake; we didn't know what she hadn't told us, and we didn't feel shorted because of that missing information. Have an outline, remember what you can, remain available for questions, and receive compliments on your performance gracefully, without trying to convince your audience that you feel you failed them by not giving a so-called "perfect" presentation.

Above all, have some fun with your book talk. Although you may feel the only way to do a book or source justice is to read long excerpts from it, resist that temptation. Reading, despite its many good qualities, is still primarily a passive activity, and one that you must leave for your audience to pursue and enjoy. Your role in a book talk is to actively promote the book, and to engage your audience into an interaction with you about it, not to read or lecture at them. Of course short examples are helpful, but again, do your research carefully, and pick the shortest possible segment that gives the best possible feel for the material. If you truly believe in your books and the other sources you've chosen (which, as a library professional, you should), this foray into "sales" shouldn't be too disconcerting. One librarian suggests that "Enthusiasm is the keynote of my book-talks, wherever I am. I cannot imagine

life without reading, and I try to convince others to join in the fun" (Baxter 1998, 70).

Tours

Librarians provide people with information; that's what we do for a living. Is it any surprise, then, that one of the cardinal sins of the profession is to overload patrons with too much detail? We just can't help but cram our handouts and user guides with overly detailed instructions. That is a habit that you must curtail when it comes time to give a tour. Heeding Strunk's timeless edict to "Omit needless words!" will never serve you better than while giving a tour, where an upper time limit of twenty minutes has been suggested by many of the professionals in the field.

In addition to imposing a time limit on the tour of your library, portion of the library, or other facility, it is also a good idea to restrict group size. When you have been asked to provide a tour for a group of people, insist on scheduling multiple tours for smaller groups, rather than one tour for a large and unmanageable number of people. For drop-in tours, where you have no control over the number of people who show up, try to have a backup plan worked out with your colleagues, wherein two or more of you could split the large group and give separate but concurrent tours, or leave half the group with a co-worker for a quick demonstration of the library's online catalog while you take the other half on a quick tour, and then have the two groups switch places. If those solutions are beyond your staffing capabilities, and you find yourself facing a larger-than-average audience for your tour, do the best you can and trust that your thorough planning will help you get through it successfully.

Plan your tour carefully and — keeping your maximum allowable time in mind — show and talk about only those areas that most of your audience members will be interested in or may use. A group of retired former business professionals should suggest to you a focus on the area of your library with financial tools and periodicals (for example, ValueLine, Morningstar, *Wall Street Journal*) as well as an overview of other common fare such as the nonfiction and fiction sections and the consumer research information; in contrast, you're really not going to need to show any of those things to a class of third graders and their teacher. Plan the route of the tour logically so that it starts from a centrally located entrance point and ends near that same point (which is probably also, helpfully, the exit). Just as you cited main points for your other presentations, jot down some of the key areas of the library you'd like to show and talk about, and then walk at least a couple of different routes around them to find the most comfortable route for the journey.

On the day or close to the time of the tour, prominently post a sign or other indicator of where the tour will start (that is particularly important for tours of the drop-in variety). Nothing is more frustrating to a patron who has chosen to spend his or her valuable time learning abut the library than forcing them to wander about, wondering where the tour will be starting, and whether it has already begun without them. Post a sign as close to the front door as you can and stand by it, wearing some kind of identification on yourself, at least five minutes before the tour is scheduled to begin. You may feel somewhat foolish wearing a button or name tag and loitering in your library's vestibule, but it's not like you don't have a reason to be there. Helping your patrons feel welcome and assured that they are in the right place should be all the motivation you need to overcome your fear of dawdling in public.

Greet your tour participants cheerfully and start the ball rolling by asking them questions. What are their names? Why are they attending the tour? What are some of the things they hope to learn about the library? All of this information, while helping to pass the time before the tour starts and signaling your enthusiasm for taking them on the tour, might yield valuable suggestions for parts of the tour they might particularly enjoy. Taking that time will also give you a chance to spend a few minutes after the scheduled start time of your tour to linger by the entrance and welcome any slightly less punctual attendants (I've been that less punctual attendant, and I was always grateful when I could still join the group with a minimum of fanfare). As you begin to follow your route, do your best to maintain eye contact and a conversational tone with the group members; often, that means stopping the group in various places to talk to them about the specifics of those places. With more experience and a good feel for where the footstools and book carts are in your facility, you may be able to walk backward and speak with the group while you're on the move, but if that's not on your list of skills yet, be warned that it's very hard to talk over your shoulder to a tour group. Doing so makes it very difficult to maintain eye contact, concentrate on what you're saying, and be heard. For the most part, you will want to move as quickly as possible to certain spots, then halt the group while you talk about points of interest and answer questions.

It's often a good idea to break up the monotony of a tour by combining it with a short demonstration or other presentation, or even the introduction of other staff members, who might speak briefly with the group to provide a break from your voice and presentation; variety is a good trick to keep participants interested. Introducing staff at the circulation or reference desks can be a nice way to personalize the library, and to allow others the chance to speak to the tour group about what their area is all about and how they can be of assistance to the participants. Of course, that necessitates checking with said staff members before your tour starts; at the very least, make it a point to let all public service staff know that a tour group will be coming through, and do consider asking them if there's anything they'd like to show or talk to the group about (for this kind of assistance, professional courtesy dictates approaching those colleagues some days before a tour is planned; it's your job, then, to figure out who will be at each proposed site of your tour on any given day). Completing the tour with a short demonstration or by providing some other sort of product (a business card with the library's hours and reference e-mail address, a bookmark with short tips for searching the catalog, a quick reference card for other software or database productions) always provides a nice bit of closure for you and the tour's participants, as opposed to simply arriving back at the exit, thanking them for attending, and then allowing them to wander off with no final proof that they ever attended the tour.

Chapter Summary

What is the definition of a teaching librarian? Sarah Leadley describes the job and the person: "This individual often receives little or no formal preparation for the responsibilities of teaching, has few opportunities for continuing education, struggles to balance teaching with his or her other responsibilities, and to top it off, tends to be susceptible to burnout" (Leadley 1998, 104). That's a daunting fate, but it need not be yours. Thorough research and preparation, as well as an ability to imagine your audience's needs and questions, are vital skills for librarians who engage in small-group instruction. Realistically develop your lesson plan objectives and list ways to achieve them, so that you can be ready to address the variety of learning styles your students will bring to the session. Try to make your teaching as active as possible by customizing your presentation to your workshop attendees and interacting with them. that can be achieved most easily by speaking extemporaneously (from brief notes or an outline) and adapting the speech on the fly, as necessary. Always remember that one of the most important parts of instruction are concluding your workshop (or class, or book talk, or tour) with an offer of further availability, as well as sending useful resources and handouts with your audience members to help ensure their satisfaction with your session.

Always enjoy yourself. If you're enthusiastic about what you're teaching or demonstrating, you will naturally encourage your class or patrons to match your level of enthusiasm. Providing some kind of instruction or presentation is a job duty that is going to be more present than ever in all librarian job advertisements. Already, "a perusal of recent *College & Research Library News* and *American Libraries* issues reveals that all academic reference and public services positions included substantial instruction responsibilities" (LaGuardia et al. 1996, 17). Teaching is a skill that we would all do well to cultivate.

Further Reading

Day, Ruth S. 1980. Teaching from Notes: Some Cognitive Consequences. *New Directions for Teaching and Learning* 2:95–111. Although written to help instructors (university and college professors, for the most part) learn a variety of ways to prepare and speak from lecture notes, this excellent study provides a helpful overview of different speech outline formats (such as reading from a verbatim script, a major points outline, tree diagrams, pictorial or graphic notes, and hybrid formats). Any speaker wishing to learn the advantages and disadvantages of different speech preparation notes would do well to consult this article.

The Information Literacy Instruction Listserv. Martin Raish created the BI-L listserv in 1990 to provide a discussion forum for bibliographic instruction and other public services librarians. Recently the list moved to its new permanent home on the American Library Association's server, as part of the Instruction Section for the Association of College and Research Libraries. I myself am greatly indebted to the professionals who contribute to this listserv; it always features insightful articles and discussion, as well as practical tips and pieces of advice. For more information about the list, to search its archives, or to subscribe, please visit http://bubl.ac.uk/mail/ilild/.

LaGuardia, Cheryl, Michael Blake, Laura Farwell, Caroline Kent, and Ed Tallent. 1996. *Teaching the New Library: A How-To-Do-It Manual for Planning and Designing Instructional Programs.* Vol. 70, *How-To-Do-It Manuals for Librarians.* New York and London: Neal-Schuman Publishers. An extremely practical manual including chapters on becoming better teachers, designing and gaining support for information literacy programs, and suggestions for teaching in cyberspace.

McKeachie, Wilbert J. 1999. *McKeachie's Teaching Tips: Strategies, Research, and Theory for College and University Teachers.* 10th ed. Boston and New York: Houghton Mifflin. I have a CD (*Can't Have Nothing Nice*) by a band named the Gear Daddies, and in the liner notes, the disc's producer states that he will "never, ever, love a band the way he loved the Gear Daddies." I've read a lot of teaching manuals, but I will never, ever, love a book the way I love *McKeachie's Teaching Tips.* It is, hands down, one of the best sources for learning how to teach students (ostensibly it's only for those teaching at the college level, but the tips seem universal enough to consult when teaching anyone). Although not all of the chapters will be applicable to librarians (we very rarely have to give tests, after all) the chapters on improving lectures and discussion sections should be required reading for all information professionals who are facing the challenge of instruction.

CHAPTER 10

Meetings

Have you ever thought about the absurdity of pulling people off service desks
so that they can attend a meeting on how to improve service to the public?
— Will Manley, *Uncensored Thoughts*

Whether you consider meetings the curse of your existence or the only way to achieve consensus, the simple fact is that the library world involves a lot of them, so it will be to your advantage to learn how to survive them. If you dislike meetings, you may find useful information here to make the meetings you attend more useful to you; if you're a fan of meetings, you may find ways to more often achieve what you already view as their teamwork-encouraging purpose.

tion; and (5) Keep the discussion on track (Lucas 1998, 422). Catherine Sheldrick Ross and Patricia Dewdney state that "Groups may be further described in terms of their purpose, duration, size, personality, and communication structure." (Ross and Dewdney 1989, 138). Both agree that small groups must balance at least two functions to be effective: the task function (what gets done) and the maintenance function (how it gets done). We will now focus on those two tasks.

Before There Were Meetings, There Was Small-Group Communication

There are many ways to view the challenge of communicating well in small groups. Stephen Lucas posited that members of small groups share five responsibilities: (1) Commit yourself to the goals of your group; (2) Fulfill individual assignments; (3) Avoid interpersonal conflicts; (4) Encourage full participa-

Getting Something Accomplished: Your (Not So) Hidden Agenda

Nobody, whether they are the facilitator of the meeting or a participant, wants to feel that their time has been wasted. To avoid that, it is imperative that all groups have the first and common goal of accomplishing what they have been charged with doing. The first step toward reaching that goal is to make sure that everyone in the room has an interest in the proceedings and is committed to doing his or her part to work with the other group members. In this age of networking and committees, it is tempting for librarians (especially new graduates or those who have chosen librarianship later in their work careers) to join any and all groups that they perceive may help them get to know the right people but are nonetheless groups in which they have low personal interest. On the other hand, do not make the mistake of eschewing any committee memberships that are offered to you, only because you "hate meetings." A third aspect of group membership is to recognize when you have become involved with a group in which you do not enjoy good interpersonal relationships, or that you fear is making little or no progress for the time you invest in the membership. I can promise you that no one else on your committee or in your group wants to sit next to the person who pays no attention to the proceedings, who is actively disruptive, or who does not fulfill their share of the work. A simple rule of thumb: try to serve on only those committees that appeal to you professionally and personally (when, of course, group membership is optional), and commit yourself to serving them, rather than anticipating how they will serve you.

Whether you are leading a meeting (because you are the chair of the committee, because you have called the meeting, because you are the senior staff member, or for any other reason) or attending a meeting, there are some things you can do to make it a positive and fruitful experience for everyone involved. On the way to fulfilling your goals, your group will have to gather information, discuss issues, and finally, make decisions. The best approach to move all of these maintenance tasks along is to have an agenda and to stick to it. The importance of having an agenda and sticking with it is well documented in all human resources and communication literature, and with good reason: the agenda gives you a framework for participation and task completion.

If you are leading the meeting, prepare an agenda and distribute it before the meeting. Make it clear that you expect everyone to bring it along to the meeting, and that additions to it are welcome, as long as they arrive at least an hour before the meeting starts. You may be viewed as a harsh taskmaster for a while, but eventually your expectations will come to be the norm, and if anyone needs to take notes, minutes, or other notations, they'll be glad to have a handy outline on which to do so. If something comes up while the meeting is in progress, make the suggestion to table that issue or discussion until the next meeting, when it can be added to the agenda, and again, distributed beforehand. That effectively and rightfully gives all members of the group, not just the person who has made the suggestion, time to focus their thoughts and, if they have an opinion to offer, their words on the issue. Tabling the issue may briefly upset the person making the suggestion, but you may be pleasantly surprised by the appreciation of the group's other participants, who will welcome the chance to formulate clear thoughts on new items, instead of having to verbalize knee-jerk reactions to them. If you are merely attending the meeting, abide by the facilitator's expectations regarding the agenda, or, if they regularly do not prepare one (and the ensuing meetings are formless and lengthy), politely ask them ahead of time what the meeting's topics will be, so that at the very least, you can prepare your own thoughts on the subjects.

Providing an agenda or outline for your meetings can also help you to limit the time spent in them. Recognize that holding a three-hour meeting on how to provide better service to your patrons may be self-defeating if, during those three hours, you leave a single librarian at the circulation or reference desk to wait on the patrons forming queues and grumbling to one another about poor staffing. Further recognize that good things can come out of meetings, but if they haven't come out of the first hour, they most likely won't make an appearance during the third hour when everyone is getting tired and dejected because it seems that nothing is getting accomplished. When I speak in terms of hours, of course, please take these arbitrary time amounts as guidelines; different meetings will dictate different time frames. Meetings dealing with dense technical matter, such as the software requirements for library catalogs or metadata requirements for digital collections, will most likely require a substantial amount of time to be covered adequately; meetings on more ephemeral issues, such as brainstorming ideas to provide better service at the circulation desk or the number of workshops on library databases to be held during the semester, may be shorter. Nobody said facilitating meetings, which includes ending them, was easy; try to strike a balance between adequately covering the topic and everyone looking wistfully out the window.

As a committee's leader or chair, you may also be responsible for making sure that resources and assignments are being shared and completed equally. Anyone with a college education can tell you that undergraduates intuitively know that the fastest way to complete a group project is to give everyone an assignment and due date, and then the only meeting that is really necessary is the one in which the group gathers, compiles the materials, and does a bit of editing to make sure those materials end up as a cohesive product. Sadly, a lot of professionals lose that intuition the moment they're asked to work on a project with colleagues; I assure you that very little will get done if all of you insist on creating and agreeing upon every word that goes into the project. A leader's responsibility is to make sure that everyone has an assignment or job, that those tasks will be done by the agreed-upon time, and that they will be reasonably comparable in tone and quality. If your committee has been charged with the directive to endeavor that all patrons leave the library feeling that they have been served, spend some time discussing the overall goal of Values Based Circulation and then send your members on their way to gather information and brainstorm possible solutions, which can be discussed and then accepted or fine-tuned at the next meeting.

Leading or facilitating a meeting is not the only way to have an impact upon its degree of usefulness. If you are not in a position to lead, find another active way to participate, such as volunteering to take minutes, or to set up the AV equipment or run a computer presentation while someone else is speaking. Much like volunteering to speak, volunteering to do these other less-than-popular jobs will not only gain you the appreciation of anyone who doesn't want to take minutes, it will help you indicate to your colleagues that you are a person who is willing to do anything to make everybody else's working day go smoother. It's not the worst image to cultivate, particularly if you do eventually get to direct meetings and you can face a group of people who may remember the lengths you went to, personally, to help them. The golden rule still does apply; do unto others in meetings as you would have them do unto you.

So when leading meetings, it's really just a matter of being prepared, and not overstaying your welcome. When attending or participating in meetings, use the time to listen actively (a strategy outlined in chapter 1) and do whatever you can to help others (and, inadvertently, yourself).

Leading Meetings, Start to Finish

The first part of this chapter addressed basic guidelines for both leaders and members of committees and meetings; this section will focus very specifically on a list of suggested practices to successfully hold a meeting from start to finish. Remember that as a meeting leader or facilitator, it is your responsibility to achieve objectives in a reasonable amount of time, as well as to recognize the contributions of everyone involved: "Leaders value each employee's time as though it were their own. Leaders do not require their staff to perform unimportant work. Leaders must focus their time and the time of their staff on important issues, long before they become urgent" (Sweeney 1997, 38).

1. Prepare and plan every aspect of the meeting you've proposed.

This includes making absolutely sure that a meeting really is the best way to accomplish your goal, having a set of objectives in mind, inviting the most appropriate people to help you achieve those goals, and scheduling the meeting in a suitable location and at a realistic time.

Making sure that a meeting is necessary is generally accepted as the first step in planning. Myrna McCallister and Thomas Patterson suggest not holding meetings when the subject matter is confidential or too trivial, when something could be communicated better by telephone, memo, or e-mail, or when you perceive that there may already be anger in the group regarding the issue (McCallister and Patterson 1992, 54). When you make the decision to hold a meeting, you will also want to consider the different functions it could fulfill, including such categories as "report and information oriented, decision making and problem solving, creative and brainstorming, or training and skill building" (Leeds 1991, 238). For each category, you should formulate quantifiable objectives, such as disseminating specific information about new database subscription costs, setting a final schedule for the semester's workshops, brainstorming ways to provide virtual reference, or helping your colleagues learn how to use PowerPoint. In addition to planning specific tasks, make sure to plan the meeting in a suitable location, one that is big enough to accommodate your group and has the technological capabilities you'll need, as well as choosing a meeting time that is convenient for everyone involved and will be conducive to concentration. It will not be in your best interest to schedule a meeting immediately before or after lunch, or after three o'clock on a Friday afternoon.

2. Appraise your goals for every meeting and set a time limit for the meeting. Keep that time limit in mind when creating your agenda.

After deciding upon objectives and listing them in your agenda, think about them realistically and try to anticipate whether or not you will be able to achieve or even address all of them within the time constraints you've set. Working with a team can be advantageous because "problems or tasks that are complex often require multiple forms of expertise to complete ... people learn from the group interactions in teams, and this helps them to gain new perspectives in analyzing problems and developing solutions" (Levi 2001, 11). The flip side of this characteristic is that group interaction and learning takes time, and because concluding your meetings in a timely fashion (did you ever hear someone complain that a meeting ended a few minutes early?) should be a top priority, it's better to plan to address fewer issues. If you attempt too much, ironically, you'll accomplish less because you're more likely to alienate group members by tabling multiple discussions, running over your time limit, and causing the perception that your meetings never really get anything "finished."

3. Finalize the written agenda, copy it, and distribute it to everyone you expect to attend.

Ask participants to bring the agenda along, and indicate that additions or justified changes are welcome, as long as they are submitted at least twenty-four hours prior to the meeting. Survey your agenda, and if you will need other resources during the meeting to help you and the group achieve the proposed goals, have them ready. If, for example, you will be discussing the relative merits of certain print reference tools, it is much more professional to have them ready and available in the room when the meeting starts; if you'd like any group member to discuss past achievements of the group, or issue any progress reports on ongoing projects, or give any kind of demonstration, make sure that you ask them well in advance so they can prepare themselves adequately. Nothing is more unprofessional or rude than asking a colleague to present any kind of information without giving them adequate lead time to put together their presentation.

4. Depending upon the formality (or lack thereof) of your group, be familiar with the accepted rules of order (see the end of this chapter for a brief overview) and follow them.

No matter what the formality level of your group, recording what you accomplish at each meeting is essential; ask for a volunteer or appoint a member to take minutes or notes of some kind. Start every meeting with a "refresher"—a reading of the previous meeting's accomplishments and suggestions for further action.

5. Be the first person in the room for the meeting, adjourn before your expected time limit, and be the last person to leave.

Leading a meeting can be a lot like teaching a library workshop; once again, making yourself available to all participants before and after your presentation is one of the most effective ways to indicate, nonverbally, that you are interested in speaking *with* them, not *at* them. Being the last person out also gives you a chance to return the room to its original state, which, along with adjourning the meeting on time or early, can only be good for your reputation in the workplace.

6. If you expect the meeting to take longer than thirty minutes, provide some kind of refreshments, beverage and otherwise.

I think one of the nicest things about librarians is that they usually have an appreciation for good living, and the good life includes doughnuts.

Attending Meetings, Start to Finish

Many more people attend meetings on a daily basis than get to lead or facilitate them. I say "get to lead" them, because it can often be more frustrating to attend meetings than it can be to call and hold them; often, you don't have to do as much planning or speaking, but you also don't get to set the parameters for goals and methodology. What follows is an extensive list of suggestions for how to be a gracious, valuable, and appreciated member of any group:

1. Help.
    Really. As a member of the group, there is no checklist for you to check and recheck before attending a meeting. Simply arrive on time, and offer any help that is necessary to achieve the group's directive: arranging the room, taking minutes, running the demonstration while the chairperson speaks, offering to research or record questions and tasks for the next meeting, or above all, remaining a courteous and attentive listener throughout.

Rules of Order

The basic rule of order for formal meetings can be found in *Robert's Rules of Order:*

1. Call to order.

2. Reading and approval of minutes.

3. Reports of officers, boards, and Standing Committees.

4. Reports of Special (Select or Ad Hoc) Committees.

5. Special Orders (that is, matters which have previously been assigned a type of special priority).

6. Unfinished Business and General Orders (that is, matters previously introduced which have come over from the previous meeting).

7. New Business (that is, matters initiated in the present meeting) [Robert 2000, 25].

Very rarely, unless you are having a large and very formal meeting with your organization's top management, or with your board of trustees or public library friends group, will you need to adhere exactly to those guidelines. They are useful, however, for establishing a general order for your most informal gatherings; namely, that of a call to order, a reminder of past accomplishments, progress reports, discussion of new information and further required tasks, and adjournment. If you anticipate needing to closely follow the more formal ordering principles, refer to *Robert's* for definitions of Special (and other) Orders, as well as rules for establishing speaking turns. What may be the most useful here is a brief discussion of the types and uses of motions, which are frequently made in all meetings, regardless of their level of formality.

Motions are made to propose that the group take a certain action during a meeting. Main motions constitute the business of the meeting or organization (I move to accept the Internet public use policy, I move to create a library task force to address our need for public relations, I move that we expand our current number of drop-in workshops from five per semester to ten per semester). Three other types of motions may be made while the Main motion is being considered: Privileged, Incidental, and Subsidiary. Privileged motions address special situations during a meeting and include motions to adjourn, motions to recess, and questions of privilege (a fancy way to say that members can request that urgent matters, such as if the room is too hot or someone is missing an agenda, can be rectified immediately). Incidental motions provide structure for and address the subject of the business and meeting at hand, and include motions to divide any questions being discussed, or to Object to another motion's consideration. Subsidiary motions refer directly to the Main motions and include motions to Lay a Question on the Table (or table it), which postpones discussion or decision on a motion until a later date, or to Limit debate and call for a vote at a specified time, or to Refer the matter for further study to a committee.

Of course, that is a vast simplification of the subject of meeting order; all motions are subject to the rules of order, in which they are assigned a rank, order, and the rules of etiquette dictating whether or not they can be interrupted. For further information on formal meeting procedures, you will be best served by referring to *Robert's Rules of Order*, and flipping to the tables of rules governing motions.

Murphy's Law in the Library: Whatever Can Go Wrong, Will

As in any kind of speaking occasion, no amount of preparation, organization, or just plain luck is always going to guarantee that meetings you lead or facilitate or attend are going to run smoothly. There are just too many ways for things to go wrong, and inevitably, sometimes, they will. The important thing to remember is that anything that goes wrong in a meeting can be fixed, and recognizing potential problems is an important part of fixing them before they spiral out of control.

Most problems arise when trying to build consensus among a group of people dealing with conflict. If people could agree about everything, instantaneously, we wouldn't ever have to go to meetings, or ask our colleagues for their opinions or suggestions. Whether a leader or a participant, you must start each meeting or committee project with the assumptions that everyone will have an opinion and that all opinions have value; doing so will increase the chances of effectively completing the meeting's business. When managed properly, some amount of conflict can even lead to more productive meetings, as well as more innovative and inclusive decisions and conclusions, which can only be forged out of more disparate ideas.

Conflict has been defined as "an expressed struggle between at least two interdependent parties, who perceive incompatible goals, scarce rewards, and interference from the other party in achieving their goals" (Frost and Wilmot 1978, 9). Regardless of the type of conflict (differing opinions, personal feelings, touchy subject areas), it is most readily handled by planning and enacting guidelines for meeting interaction by the group's facilitator. If you are the leader, indicate to the group that adherence to the planned agenda is essential for all members to be heard and for your objectives to be achieved. Suggest that an informal time limit be observed for discussions of sensitive or deeply felt issues, and then work within it. Observing your audience (fellow group members) is every bit as important during meetings as it is during any other presentation; to ensure that everyone who wants to issue an opinion can, keep a careful watch on who is monopolizing the discussion, and who is indicating through body language that there is something they want to add.

Although your own opinions and emotions may be an issue, do try to depersonalize the proceedings as much as possible and foster a calm and inviting work environment. If all else fails, and time limits have been exceeded and personal words or arguments have been exchanged, suggest an adjournment of the current meeting, ask for suggestions regarding the planning of the next one, and indicate the expectation that the tabled issue will be resolved then. Sometimes the best way to resolve problems is to allow group participants to step back from an issue, get away from their own emotions, and reconvene at a time when they can better focus on the true issues at hand.

Differences in individuals' level of participation can also cause some consternation during meetings. Just as people differ in the level of their social skills, your colleagues will differ in their preferred amount of speaking and listening. Some people will participate loudly and often and inadvertently dominate the proceedings, whereas others will never say a word but still distract from the proceedings by not paying attention or not contributing. Unless you know everyone in the group extremely well, it is harder to plan in advance to neutralize the effect of meeting monopolizers or nonpartici-

pants; however, careful observation of all members' verbal and body language can provide cues for your action during a meeting.

Above all, in these situations, don't forget to use periods of silence to your advantage. If many group members are not talking, don't be unnerved by the quiet, but rather use it as a space to pose more specific questions or statements to specific group members. You don't have to single people out in a humiliating manner to get results. Instead of saying, "Claire, you haven't said much, how do you feel about dropping our round of summer library tours?" base the question on a neutral statement, give the speaker options in answering, and don't draw attention to the fact that you're asking it of a person who has been somewhat quiet: "Claire, you gave several summer tours last year, right? What do you think an advantage or disadvantage of canceling them might be?" In phrasing the question like that, you have given a nonmeeting-related reason for your questioning a specific person, and you have provided a number of different ways for it to be answered. Conversely, with participants who tend to take over meetings they are not running, allow moments of silence to follow at least some of their contributions; it's human to feel uncomfortable with periods of silence, and that feeling may encourage them to conform to the rest of the group members' levels of participation. Moving closer to or sitting near a person who tends to be verbally aggressive can also provide you with a bit more proximity to the problem, a technique that can, in turn, subtly encourage the monopolizer to follow the rest of the group's example.

Recognizing that there are distinct types of conflict that can be helpful or harmful to teams is important. According to group communication theorist Daniel Levi, "Conflicts that are healthy for a team come from disagreements about how to address task issues. Conflicts that are unhealthy for a team originate from organizational, social, or personal sources" (Levi 2001, 129). You may also learn how to better manage and utilize conflict by researching it and how it relates to other group communication theories; for example, Marion E. Haynes, author of the book *Effective Meeting Skills: A Practical Guide for More Productive Meetings*, suggests handling confrontation by clarifying objectives, striving for understanding, focusing on the rational, generating alternatives, tabling the issue, and using humor (Haynes 1997, 61).

Your Garden-Variety Conflict Isn't All You've Got to Worry About

Universities and colleges across the country offer entire courses on small-group communication methods and characteristics each semester for a reason: It's fascinating and often quite helpful to learn how people can and do interact with one another in front of other people. A basic understanding of some of the specialized problems (groupthink, undue social influence, and inappropriate behavior from individual participants) that sometimes occur in small groups can help you avoid them in your own meetings and committees.

Although you will want to encourage some level of appropriate group interaction and rules for behavior, an emphasis on following the rest of the group's example at all costs occasionally leads to the phenomenon known as *groupthink*: conformity to group values and ethics. Avoiding a situation in which the "group stifles dissent and coerces members to agree" (3M Meeting Management Team 1994, 58) is an important part of achieving goals as a group. If you sense that the group is making decisions in an attempt to get along or to finish quickly, rather than effectively and positively debating all aspects of an issue, it is your responsibility as a leader to voice or encourage differing opinions (no matter what you think of them personally); or if you are a group member, your role is to question decisions that may have been made hastily or perhaps without considering all the facets of a situation or problem.

If you have taken other steps previously to display your willingness to help achieve consensus, asking the questions now that will have to be asked eventually will help you when, later on, you're expected to put the group's decisions into action. Sometimes asking those hard questions (if you pose them pleasantly and without making personal attacks) can also be a great way to take some ownership in the group and its decisions.

In 1974, a research scientist named Stanley Milgram conducted an experiment in which he told study participants to administer shocks to other participants whenever they made mistakes in carrying out certain tasks. Unbeknownst to those administering the shocks, the "learners" (those supposedly receiving the shocks) were cognizant of the study's real purpose, and were not actually receiving shocks. That was fortunate, because Milgram found (quite accidentally; the study was originally conceived to measure learning difficulties) that nearly all participants were not only willing to administer mild shocks to other people, but "sixty-five percent continued to administer shocks even after they were informed that the learner had a heart condition, the learner had stopped responding, and they could see that the level of shocks being administered had increased to dangerous levels" (Levi 2001, 135).

The experiment helped prove that people are often obedient to authority figures even when those figures have no real power to reward or punish them (the mere idea of the experiment conductor's "authority" was enough to gain obedience from the study participants), which is an important point to keep in mind when running a meeting (for a more lengthy discussion of the experiment, visit the website http://www.stanleymilgram.com/).

The effects of social influence on group discussions were specifically addressed by Norman F. Maier, a pioneer in the field of problem-solving groups and discussion, who concluded that "Even when the discussion leader has no formal authority over the group, his position is seen as one of power. Thus a leader's suggestions are either blindly followed or resented rather than weighed" (Maier 1963, 252). Knowing the causes and effects of social influence can help you avoid falling prey to their harmful outcomes in your own team interactions.

Inappropriate or just plain rude behavior exhibited by group members can also have a harmful effect on a team's productivity. When individuals perceive they have no real function or input in a group, they often become the people who are variously referred to in the literature as the jokers, the cut-ups, the smart-alecks, and so on. We all know that person, and (I'm not proud to admit that I know this from my own experience) I'd wager that at some point we've all been that person. Someone who makes appropriate jokes or humorous comments some of the time can be appreciated for adding humor to a situation, but those who make numerous comments only to their neighbors, or at inappropriate times, add stress to a group's interaction and are often considered inattentive or rude colleagues. This is not to say that you can never enjoy yourself, or sit by your friends, or try to help foster a lighthearted approach or environment; it is merely a return to the golden rule of doing unto others in meetings as you would have them do unto you.

If you were leading a discussion, would you like to face a clique of two or three people whispering and laughing? Of course not. If you're the group's leader or facilitator, and you do find yourself facing individuals who are interacting inappropriately, consider changing your presentational or agenda style to keep their attention and display to them that they are expected to participate with one another. Failing that, strive to find similarities between you and the individual(s) so you can work to minimize your differences in the future; it has been suggested that "you get along better with people when the emphasis is on similarities between you" and that a strategy known as blending (trying to reduce individuals' differences to increase rapport) and redirecting (using that rapport to change the dynamics of the interaction) can be helpful in resolving differences (Brinkman and Kirschner 1994, 38).

Chapter Summary

By balancing the task function of what gets done with the maintenance function of how it gets done, small groups can be particularly effective for sharing information, solving problems, brainstorming creative ideas, and helping participants build skills. Those calling and conducting meetings can help ensure their expediency by considering whether or not they're truly necessary, formulating quantifiable objectives, preparing and distributing an agenda, following accepted rules of order, being available to all participants, and, if necessary, providing refreshments. Those attending meetings can aid task completion, the facilitator, and the other participants by volunteering to take minutes, assisting with demonstrations, or any number of other maintenance tasks.

Although a group's adherence to strictly defined rules of order such as *Robert's* will vary depending on the group's level of formality, some understanding of basic rules for meeting structure and motions can often help a meeting's chair conduct an organized and efficient session. Most meetings follow a pattern of approval of the past meeting's minutes, reports of Standing and Special committees, Special Orders, Unfinished Business, and New Business. The four types of motions most often used are Main, Privileged, Incidental, and Subsidiary; these motions constitute the meeting's business, address special meeting situations, provide meeting structure, and help address Main motions, respectively.

In the course of working with groups or teams, many different types of conflict can often distract a group from the work at hand. Some forms of conflict, such as disagreements on how to address task issues, may provide the impetus for good group discussion and advance their work; other types of conflict, especially those that are personally or socially motivated, tend to be very harmful to a group's interpersonal working relationships. In addition to conflict, other types of specialized problems like groupthink, unquestioning obedience to authority or acceptance of social influence, and inappropriate behavior from individuals can also result in poor decision making and action from small groups.

At their worst, as Will Manley has suggested (in the quote at the top of this chapter), meetings can approach absurdity, particularly when they consume staff members' time and energy out of all proportion to their results. At their best, however, it is important to remember that meetings can also "establish teamwork, develop pride in the group and organization, generate new ideas, provide problem-solving satisfaction, and offer leadership training" (Conroy and Jones 1986, 124–143).

Further Reading

Dewey, Barbara I., and Sheila D. Creth. 1993. *Team Power: Making Library Meetings Work*. Chicago and London: American Library Association. The authors of this book have managed, in a mere 123 pages, to provide the first and last book that librarians should ever need to consult regarding their specific meeting characteristics. From meeting goals and processes to communication theory and a history of meetings in the library world, it's a very interesting study of how librarians can and do interact in small groups.

Haynes, Marion E. 1997. *Effective Meeting Skills: A Practical Guide for More Productive*

Meetings, Crisp 50-Minute. Menlo Park, California: Crisp Publications, Inc. Because it's always a good idea to get a different perspective, consulting this book will be helpful for those who enjoy manuals that include more interactive tools such as worksheets and checklists. This very succinct and reasonable handbook asks all the right questions, such as whether or not the meeting you want to have is really necessary, and how you can use your own leadership and facilitation style to improve the productivity of meetings you attend.

Levi, Daniel. 2001. *Group Dynamics for Teams.* Thousand Oaks and London: Sage Publications. If you have any interest in the psychological and sociological aspects of how people work together and communicate, this is the book for you. All facets of teamwork and team dynamics are discussed, from team processes to cooperation and competition, and from managing conflict to decision making. Many groundbreaking communication studies and theories are disseminated here, including those examining authority and the influence of power and social pressure.

Wanden, Joy A. 2001. Making Meetings Matter! *Library Mosaics* 12 (4):8–12. Simply put, a simply great article on ten short and common-sense ways to make library meetings a little more bearable. It also provides the reader with a great bibliography for further research on meeting protocol and methodology.

http://www.e›ectivemeetings.com/. Created and sponsored by SMART Technologies, Inc. (during the course of the company's own search for practical meeting tips and advice), EffectiveMeetings.com is a good source of articles, tips, and other resources for improving organizational meetings. In addition to providing information about meeting basics, planning, and presenting, the site also includes a section on less traditional types of meetings, and suggestions for videoconferencing and other electronic meeting resources (that may become increasingly important in the library profession).

Chapter 11

Presentations to Large Groups

I recently attended a conference where out of eight presenters, only one speaker actually made a good presentation....
— Danelle Hall, "The Care and Feeding of Speakers and the Spoken-To"

We have finally arrived at the type of presentation that you might have pictured when you first picked up this book: the stereotypical picture of public speaking in the form of one speaker, facing a large audience, and delivering a highly structured and prepared speech or demonstration. Although many of the considerations discussed in the first half of this book were listed with this large-scale type of oratory in mind, a closer examination of the characteristics and challenges of speaking to large groups of people (say, more than twenty individuals) is merited.

You've Come a Long Way, Baby

The basic principles of good public speaking still apply; you will need to prepare your presentation carefully (researching and refining and practicing it), and eventually you'll have to deliver it, keeping in mind your techniques for good breathing, nonverbal communication, and word choice. When you step in front of a large audience, however, you should also be aware of that environment's unique challenges. Speaking to large groups often requires more formality in delivery and language, the use of technological aids such as microphones or projection systems, and an even more stringent understanding of the composition of your audience.

Formality Is Not Dead

Librarians have never been ones to stand on ceremony. It's hard to be formal when patrons ask you their more personal medical questions, you spend a lot of time pulling *Glamour* magazines and the swimsuit issue of *Sports Illustrated* out of the library bathrooms, and college students ask you for the botany (read: marijuana) growing guides. Speaking to large groups, however, does necessitate a little more formality in tone and word choice than one can get away with when teaching or speaking with small groups or your colleagues, simply because more audience members means a larger variety in their expectations for your performance. The most common situations in which you will be speaking to large groups include conferences and large-scale staff presentations or demonstrations. Some examples of public speaking wherein you might face larger audiences are the following:

Delivering your research or writing at a conference.

Demonstrating a new public access catalog to your university's academic library staff.

Presenting a budget report to your city-wide public library colleagues.

Demonstrating a new electronic product that you have purchased (or wish to purchase) to the members of your firm or company.

Speaking to a large group of undergraduate students at a university orientation session.

A quick glance through this short list of possibilities should suggest that these performances will be less of the give-and-take, off-the-cuff affairs than are training one new staff member or showing four high school students how to use a newspaper database. Because it is harder to encourage interaction and casual participation from a large group (although it is certainly still possible), it will be necessary for you to more carefully structure and prepare your talk. Again, you will have to put yourself in your audience's place and think of all the possible issues and questions that will be raised in the course of discussing your topic, and address them within your outline.

Speaking of your outline, organization is of paramount importance in this more oratorical situation. Not only must you carefully structure your speech, you

must also explain it to your audience. If you intend to offer a post-talk question and answer session, take care to provide a handout with an outline or summary of your main points so that your listeners can keep up with you, take notes, and get a feel for the big picture of your presentation. In addition to providing a written outline, provide a verbal one as well; after your introduction, state your main points, and then repeat them as you go along. For example:

> Today we'll be looking at one competitor in our current search for a new automation system. I will be giving a quick overview of the system's circulation module, its acquisitions module, and its OPAC user interface. I'll then show you two examples from other campuses that have already implemented this vendor's system, and we'll conclude with a question-and-answer period. I'll need a volunteer at that point to list our questions and concerns so that I can pass them along to the vendor after today's talk.
>
> We start today with the circulation module; in particular, the check-in and check-out screens, and patron request capabilities....

The constant repetition may seem unnecessary when you consider that we can listen much faster than we can speak, but it is our ability to hear much more than is being said that makes this strategy necessary. Even if your listeners' thoughts should wander (and they will, because they'll take in what you're saying faster than you can get it all said), your transition sentences introducing each facet of your topic will serve as periodic cues that they need to return their attention to you. Some of this repetition and structure might begin to make you feel a little order-obsessed, but it's better than wandering through your main points without any kind of directional sentence cues.

Speaking to large groups also means you'll be facing an audience with more variation in their knowledge levels, personal interests, ages, and any number of other factors that will necessitate more formal language. Those differences do not mean you have to write down every word you will say in advance, or choose unfamiliar or big words. You simply must be more aware than ever to avoid letting jargon, slang, or verbal fillers such as "you know" or "um..." into your talk. Just as it's advisable to go to a job interview looking the best you'll ever look for that particular job, you should face an audience looking and sounding the best you'll ever look or sound as one of them. If you are scheduled to present to library administrators at a prestigious conference, you will have to dress the part and use the appropriate tone and language. If you'll be presenting troubleshooting guidelines or software tips to a battle-weary circulation staff during a weekday training session, you probably won't need to break out the power suit, but you will need to know your stuff, and standing a little straighter or dressing a little better than usual might not hurt, either.

Some tips for projecting a more formal and professional image through your speaking style:

✓ Keep all of your points concise. (Omit needless words!)

✓ Write down key terms and definitions beforehand so you're sure to remember them correctly.

✓ Practice using brief pauses or silences between points instead of saying "mmm..." or "you know..." or "okay?"

✓ Do define long or tongue-twisting acronyms the first or second time you use them, and use just the acronym thereafter.

Although you should always prepare carefully, top-notch research and organization is vital when speaking to groups of more than twenty people.

To Amplify or Not to Amplify: That Is the Question

The decision to use a gadgets is one component of public speaking and communicating that is very hard for me to talk and write about, because given the choice, I would always perform like the actors in Shakespeare's Globe Theater — without amplification tools or presentation technology of any kind. Given the increasing reliance on technologies of all types in our profession and in society, however, the choice to speak without a microphone or a presentation software slide show is not always an option. When trying to reach a large audience, it is often necessary to use a microphone or some kind of public address system just to be heard. That is why, in addition to preparing your speech itself very carefully, you must also devote more time to rehearsal and practice. If you know the room or space in which you will be speaking, do visit it if at all possible. Make sure you have the answers to the following questions:

✓ How far away is the back of the room?

✓ Will your audience be able to hear you without a microphone, or will some kind of amplification be necessary?

✓ If the room is sufficiently small so that you could conceivably be heard without using a microphone, will you strain your voice or your throat without one?

✓ Are microphones or other amplification systems available for your use? If so, how do you use and attach or hold them? If nothing is available, will you have to bring your own?

✓ If a system is provided, can you practice using it ahead of time? If you're using your own or your company or institution's microphone, do you know how to use it, and how it needs to be plugged in or recharged?

✓ What types of presentation tools are available, such as computer projection systems or screens, overhead projectors, and so forth? Will you know how to make those things work, as well as how to use them to their (and your) fullest potential?

✓ If presentation hardware and software is available, is it compatible with things you will bring yourself? For example, what version of PowerPoint is available, and what version did you use to prepare your slide show? Will the computer accept your disk? If you need a live Internet connection, is that type of connection available and possible?

✓ Is there anyone at the facility available to help you practice ahead of time, and help you set up and troubleshoot at the time of your presentation? Or will you have to set up and navigate everything yourself?

✓ If all your best preparatory work goes for naught, and you do have technical difficulties of any type before,

during, or after your talk, do you have an alternative plan of action ready?

Answer those questions as early in your preparation time as possible so that you can adjust your style to accommodate those answers, and don't be afraid to ask a colleague or a friend to help you inspect the presentation facility and explore those questions. A colleague can sit in the back row and tell you if you can be heard, and if there's one thing I've learned from experience, it's that two heads are better than one when trying to understand and use presentation tools or hardware of any type.

If you'll be speaking at a conference or another venue that is impossible to visit in advance, make sure to ask the conference organizers, or your co-presenters, comprehensive and detailed questions like those just listed. When you arrive to speak at the conference, go to your scheduled speaking location well ahead of time and try to get in a little bit of practice with the dimensions of the room and the hardware and software tools available.

Getting to Know You, Getting to Know All About You

Although you should always try to foster and maintain a personal connection with your audience, it can be harder to focus on friendly faces and make eye contact with individuals in a large setting than it is in a smaller and closer group. For one thing, if you are speaking to a bigger crowd or audience, particularly in a conference or demonstration setting, there's a higher chance that you will be physically separated from them; on a raised platform, stage, or even by a table and projection system or a lectern. If you are used to talking in smaller and more informal venues (or if you are not used to public speaking at all), large-group oratory can feel like quite a hurdle to overcome. Much of my speaking experience comes from an instruction standpoint; for the most part, I taught workshops consisting of up to twenty students or colleagues and was most comfortable when walking around among them or in front of them and their computer workstations. Whenever I'm faced with a situation in which the use of a lectern is highly encouraged, I become extremely nervous, because I hate standing behind lecterns. Although it's harder for me to see people in the audience (and it's probably harder for them to see me) when I'm behind a lectern, I nonetheless feel like I'm on display in front of the attendants, rather than being an active part of the proceedings. So how can you encourage a feeling of "we're all in this together" when you and your audience are separated by the presentation space? How can you observe the audience sufficiently to adjust the tone and content of your information?

The answer lies in learning more about your listeners before you ever meet them. Knowing the attitude and knowledge of your expected audience is vital when researching, organizing, and developing your presentation for larger groups, rather than monitoring their level of attention, nonverbal cues, and informal and interspersed questioning during your talk (although that's still important). If you will be demonstrating a new software, other product, or procedure to a large group of your colleagues,

do you know anyone who has addressed them in the past? Have you attended other presentations with them? How many in the audience are people with whom you have worked, or work with currently? If you'll be speaking at a convention, have you attended the convention, or other sessions at the convention, before? Have you been in contact with, on the phone or via e-mail, any of the conference organizers or attendees? If you're making a large generalized presentation about the campus libraries to a group of incoming first-year students at your university, how comfortable are you with interacting with students and answering their questions?

Although it may seem manipulative to learn about your audience and spin your talk to them (or at least their personalities and interests), you must learn to think about this tactic as the best way to convey to them the most useful and interesting information possible. It is never a good idea to overgeneralize or depend too heavily on stereotypes, but it also doesn't hurt to anticipate your audience's reaction to your topic and presentation style.

Public speaking textbooks will tell you that one of the best approaches to analyze your audience is to consider demographic factors such as age, gender, racial, ethnic, or cultural background, religion, and group membership. This is not a book meant to prepare you for speaking on a wide range of topics and opinions in the world at large, and because of that, we may disregard many of the factors above. The one that merits attention is that of group membership, specifically, the professional group membership of library science and other information professions.

When considering group membership and audience characteristics, a few questions that should occur to you about your audience would include:

What is their average level of work experience and seniority?

What aspect of library work do they perform? Are they involved in public services, circulation, reference, youth services, administration, or technical services (just to name a few)?

Is your session mandatory, or is participation in it purely voluntary?

What's the word from the office grapevine about the product or service or topic you'll be speaking about? (I once read a tip in a magazine that suggested always having some sort of treat or candy dish on your desk to encourage visitors and conversation — that can be a great way to get the skinny on office opinions and politics.)

A more inclusive way to phrase that last one would be to consider the "disposition" of the audience toward you, your topic, and the setting in which you will be speaking, but we're all friends and colleagues here, so why avoid the obvious? No matter what your subject, there is often a large number of opinions and attitudes toward it that have been widely disseminated and discussed among staff members at the office, colleagues on the listserv, and friends at the institution or in the profession.

When I was an academic librarian, our institution was trying to find a new automation system to replace one that was rapidly becoming outdated. As it often is, it was widely perceived by all work groups affected (public services, acquisitions, cataloging, and circulation)

that their specific needs and concerns were receiving short shrift at the expense of the others. Let me tell you that, as a member of the circulation staff, my opinions and reception of the vendor representatives were definitely influenced by discussions and e-mails with my departmental co-workers. That was only natural and to be expected, so it should have been planned for as well. If you are working from within an institution, listen carefully to what people are talking about in departmental meetings; if you're coming from outside, try to get to know the people you'll be speaking with, or at least other speakers who have addressed the same audience, to see how they were received. Don't be afraid to contact people ahead of time with your outline and ask for opinions or suggestions, and do be sure to ask what questions they already have for you. That will not only tell you what parts of your presentation to emphasize, but it will also help you to prepare for specific questions and situations.

Chapter Summary

One person speaking to a large group of listeners is the mental picture most people have of traditional public speaking. In our profession, however, we don't often have to address many people at once; our main chances to do so are at conferences, organization-wide demonstrations or meetings, and lecture courses or orientation sessions for students. Although all the basic principles of good speaking (listening, researching, organizing, confident delivery, and responding to feedback) still apply, large-group communication often requires more formality in tone and style, more dependence on specialized tools (laser pointers, microphones, projection systems), and a thoroughly researched knowledge of the composition of your expected audience.

When you are speaking to a greater number of people, it also increases the number of individual attitudes, learning styles, and vocabularies (just to mention a few characteristics) you are facing. You may not agree with the theory of "lowest common denominator" programming that many television networks engage in (broadening a program's focus to appeal to the greatest possible number of viewers), but they do it for a reason. Without thinking of your audience as the lowest common denominator, it is still advisable to adopt a bit more structured style of delivery and speaking in order to be understood by the greatest number of your listeners. Adhering more strictly to your outline and more carefully considering your vocabulary will help you make the clearest statements and best possible impression.

Practicing your presentation ahead of time and (if possible) in the place you'll be giving it will also give you a chance to select and familiarize yourself with any speaking aids you may need, such as microphones or projection screens or systems. Depending on where you'll be speaking, you may not have any choice in the matter regarding amplification; your first obligation to your audience is to make sure they can all hear you, and you'll want to have practiced with such tools well ahead of time. If you can, inspect the space and tools beforehand, and take a colleague along with you; two heads (and four eyes and four ears) are better than one for figuring out the intricacies of software and technical requirements.

Carefully consider and research exactly who it is you will be speaking to. Typically, some sort of information about the audience will be available to you before speaking to large groups; if you're speaking at a conference, ask the coordinators of the event questions regarding the attendees; consider your colleagues and friends who have attended such conferences previously, or perhaps even spoken at them, as additional sources of information. If you're speaking at a university orientation, spend some time perusing the demographic characteristics of the incoming or previous year's students; if you're doing any kind of demonstration for a large number of your colleagues, feel free to ask them beforehand what they'd be particularly interested in learning, and listen carefully for indications of office opinions and attitudes about the product or service you'll be discussing.

Further Reading

Hall, Danelle. 2002. The Care and Feeding of Speakers and the Spoken-To. *American Libraries* 33 (5):64–65. This article offers timely and concise tips for speaking effectively at conferences, including the admonitions to check your equipment ahead of time and always having a backup plan.

Ross, Catherine Sheldrick, and Patricia Dewdney. 1989. *Communicating Professionally*. Edited by B. Katz. Vol. 3, *How-To-Do-It Manuals for Libraries*. New York and London: Neal-Schuman Publishers. Of particular interest in this very handy volume is the chapter entitled "Making Presentations." It is one of the only books in which I could find information on speaking at conferences written specifically for librarians.

Zielinski, Dave. 2002. How to Make the Most of Your Presentation Preparation Time.

Presentations 16 (2):32–38. This is a rather generic article on how to give presentations to large groups when incorporating electronic or software demonstrations, but it does raise helpful questions about how long you should spend preparing your speech, as well as offering helpful advice for making the most of your rehearsal and audience profiling time.

http://www.si.umich.edu/~pne/acadtalk.htm. *How to Give a Talk: Changing the Culture of Academic Public Speaking.* Authored by Paul N. Edwards of the University of Michigan School of Information, this is a rather nice round-up of the basic principles and techniques involved with public speaking in general (and was written by Paul N. Edwards of the University of Michigan School of Information). I particularly enjoyed the lists of "Usually Better" (talk, stand, move, make eye contact) and "Usually Worse" (read, sit, stand still, stare at the lectern) speaking behaviors.

APPENDIX 1

Interviews with Library Professionals

With the consent of the interviewees, all interviews are printed verbatim [except for emendations, added for clarity, in brackets].

Interview with Amy Crull, conducted November 2001

What was your job title?

Law librarian (at a law firm of 31 attorneys).

What type of information or library work did you perform there?

Let's see. Research and reference. Walk-in reference, phone reference. The website —[I was responsible for] maintenance of the website, and supervising of the library assistants. Ordering and weeding books. Also computer support.

How did you feel when you were asked to speak in public there, or give presentations?

I felt a little nervous. It's a little nerve-wracking–the fact that most of them [the attorneys] go to court, and they know how to talk. [When] I started preparing it, I was nervous, but once I knew what I was going to say, I didn't feel so bad.

So once you started talking you were less nervous?

Right. Once I got into the speaking part it just flowed. When you first get asked, you just get a little [nervous] ... especially if you don't do it a lot.

When you were asked to, what types of presentations did you give?

I gave a presentation using Power-Point to show them our website. We had created an e-mail that would go out to our clients, and then they'd have a link back to our website, so it was like showing them [the attorneys] what we were doing. We showed them one particular practice area, and then another practice area, so it was like an informational, "showing them what we'd done" thing. Portraying that we are technology-savvy. We also did that to show them Power-Point, because a lot of them didn't use PowerPoint, and more of them were starting to use it, so we wanted to show everybody that it was easy, that it wasn't a huge ordeal.

I would go into meetings, informal things like that, but then I would also do trainings for the secretaries. So that was presenting information. I would also go into [law] practice area meetings, and tell them the status of certain projects.

Like for the government team, the adoption team, they had their areas of practice. Those were always kind of stressful, because they had just a barrage of questions. [And a typical response would be] let me write that down and get back to you.

So for every practice area you had to give different presentations?

Sometimes. It wasn't like a normal, set-up thing, but I had special projects that I would be doing to tell them about. And then, when someone was hired, I would train them as well, but that was just one-on-one. Every new person to the firm, I'd take them through the library, and they'd get this glazed look in their eyes. I'd talk to them for a good hour.

Did you give tours of the library?

Yes.

How did you prepare your presentations, and how long did you spend doing so?

I would usually probably over-prepare, because I wanted to be ready for all those questions. I'd do an outline of what I wanted to say, and then, I wouldn't write down everything I wanted to say, but I'd write the main ideas. I would work on the intro, because I'm really bad at intro[ductions], but I'm better near the middle and the end.

Why do you think you're really bad at intro[duction]s?

I don't know. I just think it's the nerves. Intros are just always bad for me.

Right before you started to speak, did you feel nervous?

Yes.

And when you were speaking, would that abate a little bit?

Definitely. Definitely. It's just like I have to be nervous, to get up and talk, and then I'm fine. I don't know [why that] is.

Were you able to use any methods to overcome that initial nervousness?

I would just talk to the people around me, and not look at my notes. Because if I looked at my notes, I'd [start to wonder] what was I going to say about that? The easiest way was just to talk to people.

How were you usually most comfortable speaking? From note cards, from a written script, or other method?

[Something] like an outline. Usually I just took a piece of paper with an outline on it, but ended up not really looking at it. It just was nice to have it. I mean, think about that, with teaching. How often do teachers ever look at a note card?

So it's just to have something up there with you.

Yes. Just to make sure that if I completely blanked, I had something.

Did you often use PowerPoint, or do live presentations?

PowerPoint. Again, just to show it to the firm. I never went live with the internet. I would set things up so the Westlaw [representative] could go live, but I never did. I guess I didn't have the need to. I didn't want to make it look too complicated for anyone, because then they wouldn't necessarily use it. I don't think I used anything else, really.

When you used PowerPoint, what do you think were some of the advantages and disadvantages of a software like that?

I think people are still kind of enamored with it, they look at it like, "wow, the words are flying in." I kind of like it because then they're looking at the information and they're not necessarily worried about my delivery as much. I guess [using] it actually tends to lower my nerves, because I see them looking at that, and looking back at me, and it's not like [it's] all me. But, I think after the first couple of slides, they tend to glaze, I don't know if they're seeing what you're really giving them. So I like to keep it short.

Did you find it hard to learn?

No, it's pretty easy ... like the technical part, setting it up ... we would sometimes have problems with it, but luckily, the computer [person] would help me with it. One time we were setting up for a meeting, and our computer [person] was on vacation, and he had a DVD instead of a CD in there, so we couldn't get it to work. So the technical part of it can be a pain.

Did you ever develop handouts, or visual aids, for your audiences?

Yeah, for the PowerPoint, I made like a cheat sheet, with commands that they could do to start a presentation, animation, and stuff. And I made it very straightforward. Any handouts like that just really had to be bare bones, because they [didn't like] reading anything that was long.

Was it hard for you to pare the information down like that?

Yeah, I started out with it really long, but then you would do just the bare minimum, just so that when they walk away and forget everything you've said, they have that one thing that they might keep. Oh, [and I printed out copies of the] website, because they always wanted to see what the website looked like, and what the e-mail looked like, that was link-ing back to our website, in hard copies as well, for some people who just [are used to getting] everything in hard copy.

If audience interaction or discussion was required, anything where you had to interact with people, how did you initiate or facilitate that?

Well, like that one presentation I did, for the email and the website, [I asked them to] ask questions while I was going. It was formal but yet it was pretty informal, just because I really wanted them to get it. You know, that audience, if they can't ask a question, then they feel like they're not learning anything, so that was good. But then when I was going to meetings, I would present what I had to say, and there they were just jumping in and asking questions.

So they were usually an audience that had questions and wasn't shy about asking them?

No. So I had to be really prepared for what I was going to say. Questions are a big part of my [presentations] ... there was always some continuous thing I was reporting on, so the questions then came on what I was going to present at the next meeting.

You said earlier that you over-prepared, but when you think about answering those questions, did you still think you had over-prepared, or did it turn out about right?

Usually turned out to be about right. Usually I would ... if you didn't know some things that they wanted, I would just write it down and say, "I'll get back to you," and then [it's important] you get back to them immediately. "I'll go back, I'll send you an email."

So they expected that immediately?

Yes.

Did they have any problem with that?

Oh, no. As long as they got it right away.

Did it ever happen that a person was [somewhat] dominating, in a meeting?

Oh, definitely. [At my workplace] they have team leaders, and then they would always have the most questions. But everybody would look to them to ask questions. And then there were other people who were just there [who didn't ask questions], who didn't know why I was there, didn't know why I was brought in, they were never going to use the website.

Are there any other speaking tips or techniques you use that you'd like to share, or thoughts on how librarians in general communicate, with audiences or amongst themselves?

I think, like watching [the Westlaw representative], she's just like, beyond [good], really. At the same time, though, just [don't] be afraid to get up and talk. Be really prepared. She's (the Westlaw representative) so prepared, she's just expecting any question. You know, if you give the same presentation that's easier. When we used to do those bibliographic instructions [in library school] with those [university] librarians, you could just tell they hated it, and they were nervous about it. I would say, just hop into it, but a lot of people don't like speaking in public. That's what I found I gravitated more towards in my job, it didn't start by going to meetings, but that kind of evolved. So, I guess I liked it, because I wasn't just in my little corner, you know? I was actually going out and telling them what I was doing. So I liked it, actually.

Do you think that, as you were asked to more meetings, you liked it and they could tell that, so they invited you back to more?

Probably, yeah. I think they were more after the information, by asking me the questions, then they could move [the projects] along. But it was also to get my position more in a position of, [fewer] secretarial [duties]; they were moving that position more towards that kind of thing [speaking].

So there was a link between how much speaking you did and what the outcome of your job was?

Yes. Everything from the training one-on-one to going to their attorney monthly meetings. [It did seem like] the more I talked, the more value they saw in the job.

Do you feel it was an advantage, then, to like speaking?

Definitely, yes. They would have much rather talked to me face-to-face than by e-mail or phone. For some things e-mail was quicker, but for the bigger projects … maybe it was the field I'm in. They're [the attorneys] really just talk-oriented people, which is nice, I mean, then you have contact with them. You're not just sitting down there filling requests, and sending them off.

Any other thoughts on how librarians communicate, from conferences or meetings with other librarians?

Yes, I would go to the Wisconsin Law Librarians' [meetings]. They all seemed to get along really well there, but I didn't have a close connection to any of them, really. I take that back. I had one connection with the state law librarian, because I would always go over there when I first started, and she would show me everything. She was really nice. But the other librarians … I didn't feel close to them. Except like one time I called the UW [University of Wisconsin] Law Library, and I said, "an attorney needs this in fifteen minutes, she's going into a meeting with her client, she has to have this article, it's not in Westlaw, can you just fax it to me?" So he faxed it to me and I thought, that was really nice, librarian to librarian. [Then] a fifteen-dollar invoice came in the mail, and I thought, oh, they didn't even tell me there'd be a price, so I guess I was just supposed to know that. I can't say that all the time, because if I had a question, I could call the state law library, or there was one other librarian at Quarles [and Brady] that I would call. She was really good on Westlaw. Oh, and there was also an email list, for the Wisconsin law librarians, and then the national law librarians' email list. This one time, [an attorney] was going into this utility contract, and we didn't have the book, and I emailed [the list], and within twenty minutes, I had all these people saying "I'll fax it to you, it's twenty pages, is that okay?" That list was unbelievable for anything obscure. So that was nice, and that really helped, because they always needed it so quickly. So they're really good with email ... they're better with email than they are with calling them, I would say, law librarians. Because they're just always on it, I guess. I really relied on [the Westlaw sales representative], a lot, she did all the Westlaw training, unless it was a one-on-one problem for someone that I would help them with. She would come in, and I would set up for her to do the training, which was really nice. Once a month she'd come in.

Interview with Laura Moss Gottlieb, conducted January 2002

What are your current job titles?

I am currently a reference librarian at the Hedberg Public Library in Janesville, where I work twenty hours a week, and I'm also a freelance book indexer. I've been a public librarian, off and on, for thirty years (actually, more than that) but thirty years. I've been a freelance book indexer for twenty years. I've been a continuous freelancer for twenty years, my public library experience is more checkered (laughs). I've actually worked in public libraries for about fifteen years, I've been with the library [field] for thirty years, off and on.

Did you start in public libraries?

Yes. I've been a public librarian in major city central public branches and in small town main libraries.

Could you describe, a little bit, the types of library or information work that you currently perform?

I basically am just a reference librarian, I help people find information that they're looking for, I help them use the internet. I don't do a lot of reader's advisory because that's taken care of at another desk, wish we did more [reader's advisory].

You have a separate desk for that?

No, we have a service desk, which is the first desk everybody comes to, and then gets directed to the bathrooms or the bestsellers. That's where that kind of work gets taken care of.

And what kind of indexing?

Back of the book indexing is what I've done primarily. I've done some periodical indexing, but not much. I specialize in scholarly books, in the humanities; I have done some trade books and some textbooks, but mostly academic, and I've done scholarly books in the social sciences, but I don't enjoy that and I don't do that anymore.

How would you say you feel when you're asked to speak in public or give any kind of presentation?

Dread. You've heard this before.

Yes, it's very common.

I hear that most people would rather die, no kidding, than publicly speak. You know, there's statistics out on that.

When asked to give presentations, what type are they?

In this job I'm not asked to give very many presentations. In the past I ran a book discussion group, a monthly discussion group, at the main branch of Pittsburgh's public library. That wasn't so much presentation as more a discussion. I did do some book talks, I was asked to go there and give groups book talks. In this job I could do computer teaching, but I haven't volunteered to do that; some of my colleagues do that. I'm much better one-on-one, at least that's what I understand more. I have also taught at the college level, English, and that was a more tutorial setting, which I much preferred. I have also taught in the classroom and I didn't like that. Freshman comp.

And that wasn't something you enjoyed.

No.

Was it the subject matter or the one-to-group aspect?

Both. I don't think you can teach people in a compulsory setting, who don't want to write, how to write.

I can see where that would be difficult. When asked to speak, Laura, how much time do you preparing your presentation?

Lots.

And do you have any certain method for, when you gave a book talk, was there any way that you approached it?

I should tell you about all the presentations I've done, actually. I've done the book discussions, I've taught in school, I've given three public speeches. One was to accept the award that I got for indexing, at the American Society of Indexers convention, one was, oh, both of my sons became Eagle Scouts, and when one of them became an Eagle Scout, I wanted [to speak]. I had been very active in the troop, and I wanted to talk about what the troop had meant to us, in terms of helping us raise our kids, so that was another speech I gave. Oh, and I recently spoke at a colloquium at the (UW-Madison) library school. There were a couple other minor speeches. I've done a couple of presentations in class about my indexing, or at the Wisconsin chapter of ASI. The one for the Wisconsin chapter of ASI was about winning the Wilson award, about what [the award] was. When I talked at the university, I think it was to a class on reference, I'm not sure. The colloquium was on homemade, library-made indexes.

Those must have been pretty good-sized groups; the ASI convention?

Yes, and I got to do an index-signing, how often does that happen?

When you had to talk to the ASI convention, how long did you prepare that, since it was a [more] formal thing, I would guess?

Yes, but it was all, it was my personal feelings. I find it easiest to talk about my personal outlook on things. And really, that's been the unifying factor in all my most successful speeches, that I was talking about my own ... something I really cared about. Unlike Freshman English, which I also do care about, but not, well ... those [classes were more] packaged kinds of deals, where I taught, they were all prepared. I didn't have the, you know, first you have to do the compare-and-contrast paper, then you have to do the ... there wasn't any room for creativity.

Not in the compare-and-contrast paper? (laughs)

Well, you know what I mean. I like to talk best when I feel like I can really say something about something that's important to me, something that I can talk about [from] my life experience.

When you say you take lots of time preparing these, do you usually sit there and work on it?

Let's talk about the colloquium, because that's the most recent one. [A UW professor] asked me to do this, he was a professor there, he must have asked me last summer, probably in June, several months in advance, and he told me it would be in November. And I started thinking about it for a long time, about what I would say, what I could say. He said I could talk about any subject I wanted, so I started out [thinking]. I had to give him a title right away, so I gave him the title "Indexing in the Information Age;" I figured that would be broad enough to cover anything. But then, at work, I started creating an online database for the local newspaper, basically turning a clipping file, [our] newspaper clipping file, into something like a database. And then I started thinking about how many libraries really do this kind of thing, and they never think of it as indexing, and librarians don't credit themselves, they don't take enough credit for imaginative and useful homemade indexes they make. They don't even call them indexes, they call them files. But anyway, I started focusing on that kind of thing, and then I found more and more examples from different libraries,

and examples from my library. But then I really, really, wanted to start it out with a bang, I had in mind pretty much the content. But I figured everybody, you know, most people start with a joke, and I'm not much [good at that]. I love to hear jokes but I'm not a very good joke-teller, so I decided I was going to wear this outrageous outfit that I had bought for a wedding, which was a rust-colored, shiny, pantsuit that has sparkles all over the top, and I opened by talking about expectations, where people have expectations of librarians. [This idea was based on] when I was a freshman at the University of Wisconsin, in 1968, I heard that Germaine Bree was going to come to speak, I don't know if you know who she is ... she's a very distinguished French professor. You have to remember that I was eighteen years [old], and I had never met a woman scholar, never seen one, and the only thing I knew about her really was she had been Albert Camus's mistress, and I liked Albert Camus's work, I thought he was wonderful, and my vision [of] what she would be like, I really thought she was going to come in a pink negligee wearing a pink boa. Yeah, my expectations were all shaped by Marilyn Monroe. So in my presentation, I used overheads for the very first time in my life, and I had a picture of Marilyn Monroe, and I said, this is what I expected, and then I showed another overhead of what she (Germaine Bree) really looked like, which was a woman in her sixties with black glasses and steel-gray hair and a severe gray suit, and she was just so erudite, and so impressive in every way, but not particularly as a sexual icon. And I was just so excited by this, because to me, I really had thought that women had to make a choice between being Marilyn Monroe, or being

Germaine Bree, in her reserved gray outfit. So the point I made using that example, was that, I know what their expectations of a librarian was, in that audience. I also wore all my rhinestones, and I said, "I want to make the visual point that contrary to those expectations, indexes and indexing is what makes a work really sparkle, what makes library service, lifts it above the average, because you can find things that nobody else can find." So, then I was very happy, once I had come up with my story. That was the hardest thing, but once I came up with it, it made me very happy, because it tied everything I wanted to say together, and I thought it really would make an impact that nobody would forget. And I was able to tie it all up at the end and get back to my original story, so that made me happy.

And one of the things about being a freelancer.... If I had been a representative of my library, where we have a dress code, I would've thought that I would have had to wear my steel gray suit, which I don't even have, but I would have had to look professional, and it was very liberating to be able to come as myself, my silly self, my wilder self, and as a freelancer, to say "this is my experience," and not have to worry about having this professional image. To me, anything other than jeans is a costume. And if I'm going to wear a costume, I might as well wear the most outrageous one I have.

Do you feel nervous before you start to speak?

Yes, I do. Actually, I feel most comfortable having a speech written out, and I do read it most of the time. I should try to get away from that. Once I have it written, and I've practiced it, and practiced it, and practiced it, I've practiced it a million times ... like I said, I'd never used an overhead projector, much less PowerPoint, so I went in and practiced with that. Once I've done that, then I really do relax and I actually enjoy talking. It's the dreading and the lack of preparation that I dread.

So once you start speaking that abates?

Yes, and even a bit before, if I feel prepared. It's a powerful position, speaking, isn't it? You control everything. For example, when I gave the colloquium, I forgot to give the title of the paper until I was in the middle, but by then I felt I had really won them over, so it was no biggie.

How are you most comfortable speaking, from notes or an outline, or another way?

From a written speech that I prepare and read, and have practiced, practiced, practiced.

Do you find you're able to maintain eye contact while reading, because you've practiced it so much?

Oh, yes, I get to know it well enough that I can look up, and when I use an anecdote, I try to break it up by looking around and not just reading it.

Do you often use software like PowerPoint, or do live technical demonstrations?

No, I don't use PowerPoint. I wouldn't mind learning but it's not too likely that I will. When you think you're only going to give two or more speeches, you don't have the motivation. Overheads worked beautifully, for my presentation. PowerPoint probably would have been better, in color, but I was happy with my picture of Marilyn Monroe and I was very happy with them.

Do you usually develop handouts, or any kind of visual aids for your audience?

No. I don't know, I hate handouts myself.

Oh, why so?

What I really dislike is when [you're given] the whole PowerPoint presentation on paper, they're supposed to be these paperless presentations, and then you get handouts of the outline and main points but not the supporting evidence, [or] the other kind of talking that in general, the [more] personal information, that's interesting. When I won the award for my indexing work, I worked in such total isolation, like you do in your room or your attic, in such total obscurity, that I was really happy with the national recognition. The Eagle Scouts, the other presentations, were really personal and not ones that leant themselves easily to handouts. I will say that I've brought two of the three audiences I've had to tears. Most of my speaking has been deeply personal, except for teaching, where I liked the subject personally but I wasn't as attached to it.

If audience interaction or discussion is required, how do you initiate or encourage it?

The book discussions were that — I didn't want to lecture, but sometimes it's hard, especially with books I didn't know. I remember one time, we had the *Gulag Archipelago* by Alexander Solzhenitsyn, I didn't know much about it or Russian history, but somebody in the audience was really into it and he kind of took over, which isn't always the best either. I do try to encourage them to do the talking.

Are you comfortable asking specific people questions to get the discussion going, if no one's talking?

Yes, or I try another question to get people started discussing.

Are there any other speaking tips or techniques you use that you'd like to share, or any other thoughts on how librarians communicate, with each other or with anyone else?

What I would say, in my very limited experience, is that I'm best when talking about things that mean a lot to me, or subjects that are close to my heart. If you don't have that conviction, I think audiences pick up pretty quickly, and see when you're just going through the motions. When I have strong feelings I enjoy it … it's [indexing by librarians for libraries] a dull subject, but if you're interested in it and it's personal the audience will listen for 20 minutes. And don't go too long.

Interview with Dineen Grow, conducted November 2001

What is your job title?
Library Services Supervisor.

How long have you held this job?
Since 1984.

Could you describe the type of library or information work that you currently perform?
It's really a mix. I do a lot of personnel work since I've got about thirty front-line classified staff members that report to me, so it's a lot of supervision, a lot of personnel [communication]. I also serve as a kind of a campus liaison for the Voyager system circulation functionality, and other libraries, where people have questions about patron records that don't work or item records don't work or any of the bigger [technical] questions as to, do you need to purge

programs, things like that. I'm usually the person who spearheads those kinds of committees. I also do a lot of public-service work, my areas involve the circulation desk, stacks maintenance, security, the circulation office; we have an awful lot of public interaction.

When you are asked, in the line of duty, to speak or give a presentation, how do you feel?

It depends on what I'm being asked to do. If it's something I feel very comfortable with it's not a problem at all and I look forward to it. If it's something that I feel shaky about, or if it's something I've never done before I can have a mix of both, "oh, this is exciting because it's something I can do differently," and "oh boy, am I going to screw this up?"

Do you get asked to do things more often that you're very familiar with, or do you get [asked] more often to do things you're not [as familiar with]?

Again, it's kind of a mix. Typically, it'll be like a new service plan [to unveil]. We mentioned the call slip [service] earlier, we're going to be giving a lot of presentations on that. It's a new service that we've got to [implement], so it was a matter of really learning that module very quickly to be able to present it at GLUGM, the Great Lake User's Group Meeting, in Milwaukee. That was a little scary, because I didn't feel like I had a good enough handle on [the module] when I was asked to do it, so, there was a lot of preparation for that. It really runs the gamut, because just this year I've also been asked to give presentations on security issues, on handling problem patrons, you know.

What types of presentations are you typically asked to give?

Mostly circulation-related or training-related, really, things about the [circulation] module. I just got done doing an Access training for a bunch of circulation folk, to kind of show them how they can pull their own statistics from their desktops, and that's something that circ[ulation] folks hadn't, in the past, been asked to do. And now, we are, because a lot of the information is kind of disparate and its something that we can do immediately, and not have to wait for LTG [Library Technology Group] or some other group to do for them, so it's given them some flexibility. But they didn't have the tools; very few of them had ever used Access in that way.

And that was something where you could really show them how Access could work for them?

Exactly, right. Which is always the best kind of presentation, if people make it specific to their work, relevant to their work, they can learn a new software package at the same time that they're understanding how our own data is collected, so that makes it easier to learn the software.

When you hear you have to give a talk, how do you typically start preparing; about how much time do you spend doing that?

Again, it depends on what I'm asked to do. If it's a brand-new thing, I tend to filter it down to, "what are the key things that I want to get across," you know, can I put it in a spreadsheet? I tend to like to have things very logically set out, and [then ask myself] "What are my steps? And what is it I'm trying to get across?" And if I can put it in a spreadsheet, or have some kind of handout that I can give to them, then it helps me, [and] that's usually what I would then use to give the presentation. How much time? Again, it depends. There are some times when people say, "Can you talk about this tomorrow at the ELC Group," and you have no time to prepare, but it's something that they know that you know well, so it's just a matter of, again, asking "what are the key ideas that I want to get across?" and make sure those are written down on the 3 × 5 cards, and then don't forget 'em. And then, respond to questions. You can always flush things out during a question and answer period, so, I don't try to stress too much if I don't give them everything, because people will usually ask if they don't understand something.

Okay, so it's no set time [it takes to prepare]?

Right, it depends. Now, for the GLUGM presentation, I spent a couple of weeks before GLUGM, because, again, we spent time learning the software, which we would need to know anyway with this new service coming up. When I was learning the software, I was also conscious that I had this talk to give, and so [I asked myself] what were the things that I would want to know if I was in the audience, for the first time seeing call slip? What would be the questions I might ask? So I tried to learn those issues, you know, if someone said "what happens if this goes away, can you retrieve it?" Well, test [those sorts of things] and make sure you know. This is very cliché, but the more you know the more comfortable you're going to be.

Right before you start to speak, do you typically feel nervous?

Yes. Yes.

Very nervous?

Hm, no; it varies somewhat. Again, if I know the audience, like it's all a bunch of circ[ulation] people who have seen me make a fool of myself a thousand times,

that doesn't bother me, but if it's a brand-new group of people I haven't seen before, I typically get a little bit nervous before that. I always make sure I have water. Because it gives you something to grab onto. And the other thing that I find very helpful is, as the first couple of people filter in, to make contact with them, to talk to them, find out where they're from, especially at large conferences. [I] just try to joke around a little bit, and that helps because, first of all, it makes you forget that you're about to speak to this roomful of people. It also gives people a chance to see you talking to people as they come in, and somehow that makes it a little bit more of a bond, [to feel] you're just one of the group kind of thing.

And, while you're speaking, do you ever feel that nervousness kind of lessen?

Yes. Especially if I don't screw it up too badly in the first three or four minutes. If I don't start out well, I find that I might be nervous a little bit longer, but if I feel I've got a handle on it right from the get-go, then I'm cool. But if I trip over my own name, then, yeah, [I'll think,] "well, this isn't a good sign."

Besides water, is there anything you do right before you speak, to calm yourself down?

Again, depending on how familiar, how many times I've done that kind of a presentation, I might just quickly look over my note cards. For really big presentations that I haven't done before, I have also taped them. I tape myself [on an audio tape] doing it a couple of times, and I listen to it, and I think, "Oh my God." And I did that going to GLUGM, going to Milwaukee. I had an hour and a half, so I could just [took] my little hand-held recorder and I kept trying a couple of different ways, and so right before the presentation, I knew where I was stumbling, I knew where I was going to screw up, and then it made me much more calm when I actually got up there.

How are you most comfortable speaking? You mentioned earlier a spreadsheet. Do you usually use a spreadsheet, or a prepared script, or notes?

I tend not to use a prepared script at all. I might, for a big presentation, write out a script ahead of time, that I practice, but then I don't use it at the actual presentation. Most of the time I have an outline and very terse kinds of sentence, like, key concepts, that might be, you know, "patron records," and then I put a few things under [that heading]: "expired IDs," whatever, to remind myself what I wanted to talk about, and that I thought about ahead of time. To remind myself, what did I want to say about expired IDs?

So it's really that true outline form?

Very true. Really short little things.

And the spreadsheet works pretty well?

It does work well. I think part of it is it helps me with my thoughts, prior to the presentation, it gives me some sort of progression, so I know where it is I want to start, and what I want to end up with. I find that helpful.

Do you often use software, like Power-Point?

Never. And I will resist it, I hope, until the day I die. First of all, I'm not ever that impressed by PowerPoint presentations myself, I think it's a lot of buttons and whistles for very little return. People spend a lot of time doing it, and in doing so, I think they lose the content. As an audience member, I find myself waiting to see what the next fancy little picture is,

rather than what are they going to say. And, I don't know, I'm just not a big PowerPoint fan. It raises the ante of "is it going to work," and if it doesn't work, and that's where you've put all your eggs, then you're screwed.

But I do know that sometimes you have to "go live," with technical, with the [software] demonstrations. What are some of the challenges of that?

Well, again, if you can't get into the database, [it's a challenge]. For example, at the GLUGM presentation, there were maybe about seventy-five people in the room, and call slip didn't work. And of course, that was what I was there to present. But I had the back-up, I had the spreadsheet to show them what the screen would look like were it live, so I knew that I wanted to have that back-up with me, just in case. And I do think that's important. I had it passed out, I didn't even do the overheads, I [could just say], "here it is." That way, if people can't see from the back of the room, well, we're not losing anybody, they have it right there and they can take it home with them, they can ask questions off it, you know, whatever. I find that that's my preferred method of doing things.

So you just couldn't get into it [the call slip module] at all?

I could show the screens but I couldn't show the progression. Requests just weren't being filled. We found out later why, it was a software bug that we weren't aware of; it wasn't the system, but it was enough to throw us off. You have to just know that you can handle that ahead of time. And, either plan for a back-up, or know your material well enough that you can keep the conversation going. "Well, this is what would happen..."

That's one of the bad things that can happen. What are some of the nice things about it?

When you've got a screen right on there that you can show somebody, or you have, you know, maybe an overhead or something like that, it helps you remind yourself, you know, what you want to do; you might forget a point or you might think later, "oh, I really should mention that," and if you have it right there you can say "oh yeah, by the way, if you're looking at column 3…" It is nice for that reason.

How do you think audiences react to live demonstrations like that?

I think it's much easier for them; it does give them something to look at, they don't have to imagine so much in their heads. But if the presentation is overpowering the content, then I think you've lost them again. That's why I don't like PowerPoint necessarily but, you have to keep it simple enough [so] that it's effective.

You [discussed] a little bit what kind of handouts you use, but what sort of handouts or visual aids have you developed in the past?

Sometimes I'll give them my outline depending on whether I think that that is helpful, not always, because usually it's chicken scratch. Screen shots, of various things, sometimes, when we've done things on security or problem patrons. We might pull out pages of our manuals, things we've written up in the past, and say, "this has helped me handle it." I like to do scenarios and give them little blurbs, like "If this situation happens, these might be the things that you would want to consider." [Some issues] might be outside of my presentation, but might be more relevant to people in a different

environment than myself. One time I had to give a presentation on security to a mix of academic and public librarians. Well, Memorial [Library] is very fortunate in that we security officers, and we have a security gate, but what about the public librarians who don't have access to that, and aren't allowed access to that because they are a public library, and what can we tell them to do? So I had all these different little scenarios of tips that they might think about, you know, if they had to confront somebody. Take someone with them, even if it's just a student, just having another person to back them up is sometimes important to calm down a potentially problem patron.

That must have been quite a mix.

It was, it was. Those are the hardest kinds of presentations to do, because your audience isn't focused, so it's harder for you to be focused, and you have to keep that in mind when you do a presentation. Who is your audience? And make sure you don't leave anybody out.

If audience interaction or some kind of discussion is required, do you have any techniques for initiating that?

A lot of times, again, [it will] depend on who I'm talking to. When you do a training program, for example, you can say things like "Okay, I need to get this statistic out. Based on what we just did, the table work, what tables do I need to pull together? Who can tell me what tables we need to use to get this query?" [I can] just ask questions to the audience, that way. Or you might, if it's more of a theoretical thing, you might say, "Does anybody have a situation that's analogous to what I just described in my library?" and then just talk about it. I mean, I think people are really willing to share information, it's never been a problem to solicit information from librarians. Sometimes [it's different with] students, you know, when you're doing a MadCat workshop or something, in those cases, then I usually just point at people, and say "How about you?" Especially the people that are falling asleep in the back, or whatever they're doing in the back, not paying attention, I love to [ask those people], "You in the hat, what would you say?" It's amazing how the rest of them will perk up. It's in their eyes (laughs), all of a sudden, that scared look.

Would you say that's a little fun?

It is fun. I enjoy that very much. I figure, look, if I have to be here for fifty minutes, and you have to do the same, we might as well get something out of it.

So that's not something that has to be intimidating?

No. Not at all. No.

Very last one. Are there any tips or techniques that you would like to share, or any other thoughts on how librarians, how we communicate with each other or with other people?

Well, we touched on the idea of "Know your audience." I think another big thing, and I touched on it a little bit earlier, is to think of the presentation you're about to do; what is it that you would want to get out of it if you were a member of the audience? I think that's really key. Because so many times people are very general in their speaking. I remember one talk that I had to give, on bringing up a new system, [on how] you evaluate systems, and I got very nervous, because I was the last person on the panel to talk, and everybody else was talking about the system that they bought and how they implemented it into their li-

brary. I was sitting there thinking, if I were out in the audience, I'd think, well, how would this affect my library? And my presentation was more of "okay, if you bring in a new system, think about how your patron database is going to interact with the old patron database, and what is your interface?" so it could be much more general [and less specifically about my library]. People came up to me afterwards and said they found that to be very helpful, so I was glad, because I was sweating bullets, thinking, oh my God, did I misunderstand what I was supposed to do here? But people actually did like it, because they said they could bring something home, where they couldn't from the other ones, because they were so specific to [their] sites. So know what it is that you would want to get out of it.

Keep things about yourself down to a minimum. I always try to think of what is it I hate most about presentations, and I [dislike] when somebody goes on and on about their credentials, who they are, what they've done. I don't care, [I tend to think] "I've got an hour, get on with it." And people do that because they're nervous, and they're comfortable with that information, but really the audience doesn't care. You have to tell them a little bit, but not a whole lot. Remember that you know probably more than they do, and that's why you've been asked to get up in front of this group. And I don't mean that in an arrogant way. [Just that] it gives you a little more of a confidence, you know, that's why you're there. People really do want to hear what you have to say; there's no reason to be threatened by who's in the audience, or anything like that. If you screw up, you screw up. You know, don't worry about it so much.

I can ask you this too, it's not on the list and we probably won't put it in, but is there any way we can help ourselves at meetings? I see a lot of meetings, they're just such a big part of being a librarian, is there any way we can make sure those go better, or take a little more charge of it, from your point of view?

You mean, if you're not the chair?

Even if you are, any ways you can get a little bit more out of it, or if you aren't the chair, any way you can help it along?

Well, I think a couple of things. You have to be very aware of what your agenda is, and not let things go off-agenda. And I think that's the same thing for big presentations, too. As people start asking questions that are not really on-topic, it's your responsibility as a presenter or as the chair, to say "How about we talk about this later." One of the things that happens, too, is that you'll get people in the audience who want to show off how much they know, and again, as an audience participant, or a person in class, I remember being like, "can't the teacher just shut them up?" You know? I think that that's very important to your presentation, that you don't let someone take over, and a as a chair of a group, to say "okay, this is not on the agenda, do we want to table it, or can we talk about this in another group," or something like that. Not to necessarily get rid of the topic, but just to [defer it from] that time period, because most of the time, people haven't had a chance to think about whatever is being brought up. And then that [makes] things messy. So I really am kind of a taskmaster, just to stay on topic, and say, "okay, we're done with that, let's move on." One thing I think is very important as a chair is to [start with] something that people can react to.

If you have a huge topic [to cover] and say, "okay, we've got to bring up call slip, how do we want to do this?" [That's] really hard for people who are at the meeting, and it becomes this kind of unwieldy, "well, how about if we do this," [discussion]. But if you sit down ahead [of time], as the chair, and say, "okay, we know we're going to have to work with publicity, we know we're going to have to work with software issues, we know we're going to have to work with training," and then, [give the specific] topics, that gives people a focus. It gives them something to react to. You can [always] table things, say, "okay, this is too big of a topic, we have to break this down, does somebody want to break this down a bit further and come back to the next meeting with it?" Every meeting that I've chaired, I've had some kind of handout, or some kind of letter, and I'll say, "okay, let's pick this apart." Then you [also] have to give up ownership of it. It's not fair to come in as the person chairing the meeting, and say, "okay, I did this, by the way, everybody sign off on it." You have to be willing to give up ownership and say, "this is just a draft. What else can I add, what did I misrepresent, what else do we want to take out," and not get defensive when people start pulling it apart. That's a way to keep the group focused and I've always found that to be my favorite way of chairing a committee, and to be on a committee. If the chair does that, I'll think "okay cool, we're going to have some focus here." Because otherwise I think it is hard for people to wrap their brains around concepts that they haven't really thought of]. You know, we've got so many other things going on in a daily work day, to come to a meeting and all of a sudden be talking about some major problem, and nobody's had a chance to really think about it, [is hard]. And if you don't give them some ways to think about it, and again, I don't mean to sound like you're saying, okay, everybody step in line, but it does help them. We get lots of good pros and cons coming when you do it that way. But if you don't provide any sort of direction then people just come up with all kinds of stuff, and it becomes very unwieldy, and I find that those meetings are usually very unproductive. You walk away saying, what did we do? And I think that gets very demoralizing. So many committees I've been on, I've actually quit some committees because of "all right, we're not getting anywhere, we're spinning our wheels and we're reinventing things all the time."

Interview with Lee Konrad, conducted November 2001

What is your job title?

I'm the head of the Digital Content Group, part-time, at the University of Wisconsin-Madison libraries, and I'm also with the undergraduate library as a Computer/Media Services librarian.

Could you describe a little bit the type of library work that you do, along with those jobs?

With the Digital Content Group, I manage the proposal development and the metadata, encoding, and imaging services that make up part of the Digital Library program.

And at the undergraduate library, what are some of your duties there?

At the undergraduate library I work partly in reference and I also manage our audiovisual collection and do collection development.

Lee, how do you feel when you're asked to speak in public or give a presentation?

Generally, I'm pretty flattered that people have asked (laughs). If you want me to step back a bit, I should say that I did reference and bibliographic instruction at the undergraduate library for three or four years, so I've done a lot of speaking in that context as well.

And what types of presentations are you typically asked to give now?

These days I mostly do presentations to describe our services, at conferences and to faculty, and internally to staff. Those kinds of things.

How do you prepare your presentations, and how much time do you usually spend doing so?

It really varies quite a bit; you want me to [talk about] anything historical, like with BI?

Yeah, that'd be great.

So, when I'm teaching a class, I mostly prepare by trying to think about the topics they're going to be working on, or is there some theme? I work with a TA or instructor, to find out what the focus of the class is. And try to shape it as much as I can, pitching it to that audience but also knowing there's certain things that we want to get across, that we think are important about the libraries. And I think in the context of describing services, [or the programs I'm involved with], it boils down to what is the audience? Is it a public relations piece, or is it more, strictly informational, or are you trying to actually [present] detailed technical knowledge about the procedures and how we implement projects? So it really depends on who I'm talking to. If it's a blend of people, try and figure out what the common denominator is between them and pitch it there.

Do you feel nervous before you're about to speak?

Not very often. I would say that I sometimes feel slightly anxious, but it's really not a big part of it. I would say that going back, historically, I remember, this is back to high school, I had these speech classes, where I used to dread the entire day. I would be a nervous wreck the days that I had to give a speech. But I noticed after a while that once I started speaking, I was no longer nervous. So it's more the apprehension. I think I spent a lot of time after that, in my subsequent work life, trying to figure out ways to stem that initial anxiousness, and realizing that it's all over in a few minutes anyway, so there's just no point in getting all worked up about it. Most of it was in my head, instead of dealing with the reality of the situation. Once I figured that out, I don't tend to get nervous anymore.

Just getting used to speaking helped you? Are there any other ways you found to not be so nervous?

I think the big one is really talking to myself up front, saying, what are you nervous about, or why are you nervous? Literally asking myself those kinds of questions, and thinking it through, saying, "well, you're ready with the material, you really have no reason to be nervous," I think that was very effective for me, to start to stem some of the nervousness before it could kick in. And gradually that starts to sink in, it's just more a way of being. Now as I prepare, it's just more like I know I'm prepared, you know, I know my material, and then I'm not really too concerned about speaking to anybody else about it.

How are you usually most comfortable speaking? From a written speech, outline, note cards, nothing?

I find that I actually prefer to work from note cards or just the briefest of outlines. I feel, the more that I have to know exactly what I'm going to say, the more nerve-wracking it is if you lose your place, and the more you think about what you're going to say before you've said it, so I'd rather just know that this is the point I want to make, the bullet point, and then just be able to talk about that, off the cuff. Just have the order of how I want to approach things in mind. That way, if somebody asks me a question, or anything like that, I'm not interrupted and I don't lose my flow; it's just a lot easier to work from this basic order I want to do things in. If I get interrupted, I know I'm going to come back to about here now, and move on. It's easier to work on the fly that way.

Do you often use software like PowerPoint, or do live technical demonstrations?

I often do.

What are some of the challenges of using those?

I have used PowerPoint. I think it works well, and I do think it gives the audience something else to focus on, and if you're worried about the idea of being stared at, and there are these people just intently focused on you, having a presentation software behind you gives people something else to be looking at, if you can keep it engaging. And I find myself doing that, myself, as I watch other speakers. It's something to do, and it also reinforces what you're saying, to just have bullet points and it helps people stay focused and understand where you're going, so it serves to provide a lot of context, I think. Instead of talking from note cards, I'd rather talk from bullet points that are up there. I think it helps the audience understand, too, that you're going somewhere logically with this as well. It's very effective. I like other softwares as well, I don't know if you're interested in specifics, but....

Yes, very much.

PowerPoint is very good; Authorware is probably the biggest one I like. You can build a lot more interactivity into it; it has a higher learning curve, but it provides a great deal of flexibility and you can do more with animations and simulations and things, sort of depending on what you're doing, it can be a very good tool. PowerPoint at the very least is pretty straightforward to learn, and well worth using.

Do you do live demonstrations, things where you're actually hooked up into databases or the Internet?

That's a good point. A lot of people like to use screen shots of databases, and things like that, because they feel if they have the canned presentation, nothing can go wrong. I have done that, but generally feel it takes more time to develop that than it's worth, especially if it's a one-shot presentation. I'm more likely to just want to go out on the fly and say, if I know we're supposed to have a live connection, the Internet is stable enough that I'm willing to risk not being able to get into something. I like working with live databases, so [the audience can] get a really good feel for what it's like. I don't like doing canned searches, I like getting audience suggestions, which is why I don't tend to do canned stuff.

Because then you can't work the audience?

Yes, I think, it can be very effective to have the canned piece, because if you have the time, it guarantees you'll be able to get certain things across, but as I said, the Internet is awfully stable these days and I'm willing to risk it.

Along with your demonstrations, do you usually develop handouts, or any kind of visual aids for your audience?

PowerPoint is another great tool because you can do sort of thumbnail sketches to give to your audience as a handout, so they can take notes based on your slides. As an audience participant I find that to be really helpful as well, so I started doing that after I saw other people doing it. It helps pace everything, and it gives people a context for their own note-taking. So I think that that's a particularly good thing. Otherwise, usually I'll do web documents that I can put together with links to places that you're visiting during the presentation, things like that.

So then they have a reference with the links?

Yeah, so if they wanted to come back, like if you're doing a web-design class, and we're using a lot of examples, you know, "let's look at this site and this site and this site," picking them apart about what works and what doesn't, just give [a list of those links to] people up front so they don't have to be focused on getting the URL down if they want to go back to it. Just simple things like that.

If audience interaction or discussion is required, how do you initiate or encourage it?

That's a hard one. So I have no answer. Again, context has a lot to do with it. When students are there for a class, as a requirement, then it's often a little bit harder to draw them into things because they're not there of their own volition. So it can be a little bit trickier to engage them, and even though it's hard to do, I find it's better to put the pressure on, to put them on the spot. So rather than just throwing out open-ended questions, hoping that someone will respond, [I call] on somebody. You know, sort of the, "you look like you'd know ..." or, you know, if I don't want to do a canned search, and I'm looking for a topic, I could just say, "does anyone have a topic?" I'll probably start that way but if no one raises their hand, I've gotta pick somebody in the front row and say, "surely you must have a topic in mind, so what have you got?" That's putting them on the spot, but it also serves notice to the rest of the class that you're willing to do that, and they have a vested interest in keeping their head in the game. They don't want to be embarrassed if they happen to be called upon. It's not that you're trying to embarrass anybody, but again, I think it does help set people up to be a little bit more engaged, because they know that they risk being called on and they probably want to be prepared or be thinking about what you're talking about if that's going to happen. You usually only have to do that once before you notice it, a subtle change [in the audience]. And that's hard to do.

But you've found it to be effective?
I've found it to be very effective.

Does the same kind of thing apply when you speak at conferences? Or is that more...?

See, there again, with those kinds of audiences, generally, you have people who have chosen to be there and they often have questions. I do encourage questions. I rarely will say "please wait until the end, I need to finish." I like people to be asking on the fly, and if I can't address it right now, you know, that particular question's going to take me some time to develop, I say "I'll come back to that" or "I'll be talking about that in a few minutes." Take those kind of

approaches. But I think the audiences tends to stay a bit more engaged when they feel like this isn't some prepared address to the nation, it's supposed to be an interactive conversation we're having, and I'm facilitating it. Yes I am trying to convey what I know, but I think the more you can include the audience, have them help set the pace by asking certain questions, I think that really helps. In general, I think that when you're dealing with audiences who have chosen to be there, they're more likely to engage and want to get involved, so again, just knowing that helps make [it] a lot less nerve-wracking. I think it's much harder to deal with say, a BI session where you're sort of just told by your professor, "that's where we're going today." And I'm sure all [our] instructors face that, even though [the students] have chosen to be in college.

Are there any other speaking tips or techniques you use that you'd like to share, or any other thoughts on how librarians communicate, with each other or with anyone else?

I think I mentioned a couple of tips that I think can be effective. I think in terms of engaging people, let them know that you're going to [gently] insist on responses in some way. I really think it's [helpful] to see yourself as a facilitator. Because that's the kind of instruction we do. It's really not speech delivery, it's not, we're not giving speeches here, we're supposed to be teaching, or, supposed to be communicating something. To me [teaching] is more of a conversation or an interaction, so it should be two-way. And I think that helps the audience really warm up, sometimes just starting by asking questions. I'm not big on icebreaker jokes unless you have a really good joke, because you run the risk of that falling very flat, but, even if you just ask questions like "how many of you have done this?" or if you're talking about a database, "how many of you have used this database, just a show of hands?" It just helps start them off right off the bat, with questions, and they're engaged, you know, instead of you doing your five-minute intro and then asking them questions [in a] set context. I'm a pretty big believer in the principle of tell 'em what you're going to say, say it, then tell 'em what you told 'em. Spend a lot less time telling them what you've told them, though. [I think] if you just started talking, and started rambling, then people [would] have no context; you'd do a lot better to at least tell them about what you're going to do today. Don't hesitate to make jokes or respond to things as they're happening. My favorite phrase when things go wrong is "picture, if you will" that's a good one. If you're doing a demo and it doesn't happen, you just say "picture, if you will...." So again, make light of it and say hey, this is not working, and that's life.

Which will happen anywhere.

Yes. It's bound to happen, so just have some stock phrases that you like to pull out, to sort of lighten up the situation and let everybody know it's not a big thing. Let's see. The biggest thing is not over-preparing, I think there's a real tendency for people to do that. I think you're better off working from bullet points, just knowing what points you want to cover, and not worrying about the actual words that are going to come out of your mouth, because no one's gonna remember those words; they're going to remember your point, not how eloquently you managed to say "boolean operator." Don't put that in though (laughs).

Can anybody eloquently say "boolean operators"?

Sarah's going to strike that one from the record.

I haven't used "boolean" anywhere yet, in the book.

You can use it, if you want it.

We'll see about that.

The idea is, don't, especially if you're talking library instruction, or you know, any kind of conference stuff, unless you're the keynote speaker where it's really just your prepared remarks, keep things more as a conversation, a dialogue. It's not a new idea, but I think people's biggest fear is thinking that they're not going to be able to gain the confidence or the respect of the audience. I think you're guaranteed not to do that if you don't engage them.

Anything else?

As to how librarians communicate ... I do have some thoughts.

I would like to hear them, because there's [a lot] literature out there on it.

I think that in general, librarians have a tendency to over-communicate. That's obviously a generality. But I think that we tend to be overly concerned with "if they don't know everything, they know nothing." And I think we need to spend more time focusing on what I can teach you, these three things, in this amount of time, and point you in the right direction for getting additional assistance if you need it. Not worry so much about, "well, I didn't get you through A to Z, so therefore, not only do you not know what you're doing, but I'm a failure." That goes in to your own lack of confidence, it feeds that also. I think it's focusing on saying "what's the core of what I need to get across?" and letting some things go. You see that with our print documentation as well, it tends to be wordy, incredibly detailed. For most people, it's like, "I just want to turn the TV on, I don't need to know how it works," and somewhere in the middle there, they just want to know how to search this database and why I've chosen this database, and not every technical aspect about how the database got it's wording in the first place. We just really tend to overdo it. And I think, again, if you've got only a fifty-minute class session to teach people how to search databases, pick three or four core things that your public wants to do and let them know that if they need additional help beyond that, [you can help.] Less is more, I guess.

Interview with Margaret L. Navarre Saaf, conducted November 2001

What is your job title?

I am a branch supervisor for Madison Public Library, at the Alicia Ashman and South Madison branch libraries.

Could you describe the type of library or information work you currently perform?

Currently my work is divided between administrative and reference and information assistance to the public.

How do you feel when you're asked to speak in public or give a presentation?

My first reaction is excitement that someone is interested in having me speak, whether it's about the library or another topic. My second reaction is panic (laughs), since I never found it easy to speak in front of large groups.

However, once I start preparing for a presentation, that initial excitement usually returns.

What types of presentations are you typically asked to give?

I often give tours and presentations at the library on materials and resources that we have available. I also do outreach programs to schools and community groups, informing them of our library and the services we offer. And, finally, I also teach classes and do presentations on a variety of topics including using the internet, and I do a travel resources workshop.

Okay. Pretty wide variety, then?

Wide variety. I'm pretty open to whatever anyone wants me to speak about, I'm happy to do it.

How do you prepare your presentations and how much time do you usually spend doing so?

I prepare for new presentations by jotting down all of the points I want to cover in the presentation, and then creating note cards that I can use throughout the presentation to keep me on task. After that, I find it very useful to practice my presentation several times, preferably in front of a live person, if I can get a willing victim to listen to me. I also make sure that I'm familiar with any props or equipment that I'll be using during the presentation. That makes me feel more comfortable. The time I spend preparing for presentations varies; I can spend as little as a half an hour or less for a general overview of the library and its resources, or several hours creating a new class or a new workshop.

You mentioned that you like to practice. Is it more helpful for you to have somebody in the room, or do you practice it in an empty room to kind of work it out?

I usually practice it several times on my own to work out the kinks. And then when I feel comfortable on my own, then I like to rehearse it in front of a live person, just to gauge their reaction, see if there's something I might want to change, and just give me the experience of doing it in front of a live person.

Do you feel nervous right before you start to speak?

Yes. I generally do feel nervous right before I speak.

As you progress in your speaking, or while you're speaking, does that abate, a little bit, for you?

It does. During a talk, I usually get over my nervousness as I get into enjoying my topic; I enjoy seeing the feedback of the audience, and if I should get off track, or get distracted or interrupted, that's when I use my notes, my note cards, to get me back on task; that's kind of my security blanket.

Are there any other ways you combat your nervousness, right before you have to give a presentation, or during your speech?

Usually, right before my presentation, I'm sitting here going over my last-minute notes.

We just covered this a little bit, too, but, how are you most comfortable speaking? Usually from a written speech, an outline, note cards?

If I'm simply giving a talk with no equipment and no interaction with the audience, I do like to have the complete speech in front of me. I'm pretty good at maintaining eye contact with the audience, and just occasionally looking down at my speech. For a class, or a tour, or any presentation that includes interac-

tion with the audience, then I tend to use an outline or note cards, just because the presentation really can change, depending on reaction or questions from the audience. So I like to be able to kind of go with the flow of how the interaction is going, but the note cards just get me back on task if I'm sidetracked.

Do you often use software like PowerPoint, or do live technological demonstrations?

I haven't done a PowerPoint presentation yet, but I would like to learn how to use it for future presentations. I've seen some of our other people do PowerPoint presentations. I have, however, used the internet for several classes and workshops. These presentations involved teaching people how to use the internet, or demonstrating resources available on the internet, and I found it essential for people to visually see what I'm talking about.

What do you feel are some of the advantages or disadvantages of that kind of live hook-up with the internet?

The advantage is letting people see what it is that I'm talking about, how the computer responds. With our classes we offer hands-on opportunities. The challenge, however, is that no one can predict when a hardware, software, or communications failure will disrupt your presentation.

Do you normally try to have some kind of back-up plan ready?

Exactly. I always like to have printed material available, in case of unforeseen technical difficulties.

You mentioned that you had seen other people do presentations with presentation software. Do you find those effective, when you're watching them?

I do. And that's why I would like to be

able to eventually incorporate those in my own presentations.

What sorts of handouts or visual aids have you developed for your audiences?

I developed user guides and bibliographies for several of my presentations. I did the Children's Guide to Using the Internet for a practicum project that I did.

In library school?

In library school. I also print pages directly from the computer to show what a particular page looks like, and to highlight specific features. And I also love to show examples whenever I can, whether it's books, magazines, videos ... when I do a talk on travel resources I always like to bring examples of the different books, magazines, videos. We show internet resources.

So actual show-and-tell type things, props?

Exactly. Good word.

When you do have a handout for something, is there a certain way you like to get those to the audience, or do you hand them out while you're talking, or before the presentation, or just set them out on the table?

It depends on the situation. Something that makes sense to hand out beforehand, I think it's nice for people to have it, in hand. If it's something relating to a specific point of the presentation, when I want to make a special point of the handout, then I might hand it out during the presentation. Also, I often do have a variety of information sheets put out on a table, something that not everyone might need to have or want to have, but make other related informational handouts available at a separate table that people can browse at afterwards.

If audience interaction or discussion is re-quired, how do you initiate and encourage that?

I enjoy sharing my own opinions and experiences, and once I've done that, it seems like someone else always has something that they would like to say. I also feel comfortable directly asking someone what he or she thinks about the topic, or asking about his or her experience, and often someone who doesn't feel comfortable raising their hand, if you go up and you start a conversation, even if it's in front of a large group of people, they'll answer you and share their ideas and experiences.

Are there any cues in body language or speech, that you can tell when somebody really doesn't want to be called on, or that somebody's more open to it?

I do read people. If I feel that speaking with them or asking them to speak would make them uncomfortable, I certainly would not choose them. I would look for someone who I'd think would want to offer something. I might, if I think, if I thought maybe they had a question or wanted to ask something but were too shy, I might approach someone after the program, and just offer to answer any other questions they might have, or give them an opportunity to speak.

Especially since you have administrative duties as well, when you think about meetings, is there a way to facilitate discussion, or to be a leader in those situations?

Usually, in administrative-type meetings, it's not so much a matter of getting people to speak, it's more a matter of getting people to state their point and limit their speech. So we do, I do often, I'm the facilitator; we take turns at some of our administrative meetings, being the note-taker [or] the facilitator. Part of the job is to keep the agenda moving and to keep the meeting on track.

Are there any other speaking tips or techniques that you use, that you'd like to share, or any thoughts on how librarians communicate?

The one thought that came to mind that I always need to remind myself about is that most of my audience is not familiar with library jargon, and that is such a natural part of my vocabulary, so whenever I complete my notes for a talk, I always look for terms that I need to either define, expand upon, or change into a more commonly used word.

APPENDIX 2

The Speaker's Bookshelf

Laughter is not only the best medicine but the best revenge, although being rich and handsome and outliving your enemies are good ones, too.
— Patrick McManus, *The Deer on a Bicycle*

At long last we're back on familiar ground, in the form of book selection and recommendations for a personal library of items to help you approach public speaking with confidence. This section is designed to provide an overview of the types of books and other resources that any good librarian can turn to for an introductory story, a concluding anecdote, or just a fun fact. They are all sources I've used personally at one time or another to try to add "a little something" to a presentation, meeting, or even small talk.

In a perfect world, we (or our institutions) would be able to afford all the reference books we wanted, but I realize that personal and organizational budgets may be too constrained to provide for all of the following works. I don't own many of them myself (every time I'm in a bookstore I caress the *New York Public Library Desk Reference* and think about selling my plasma for the cash to buy it), but for the most part they should be obtainable from any public or academic library system. They can be invaluable resources, and as such, would merit a work

expense designation; rather than spending money on a conference you're not enthused about or a workshop that you think will be less than challenging, consider asking your superior, director, or colleagues if a small amount of the money or grants typically designated for staff development activities could go to start a small collection of speaking resources. Many administrators will freely spend money on computer manuals for their staff, so it is your responsibility to suggest that books to aid communication are at least as necessary (not to mention less easily outdated).

That said, the ideal public speaking library would include at least one of each of the following types of resources:

An anecdote collection or speaker's companion.

A book of quotations.

A desk reference or companion.

A book of lists, either generalized or in your subject area.

An almanac.

A book of librariana.

Any specialized trivia or "fun fact" book (or website) in your subject area.

For each of these categories, I've listed several suggestions, and both books and websites are included; for those of you with severely constrained budgets, the websites in particular can provide a wealth of freely available information. I've also provided examples of how each source could be used in a hypothetical situation.

Anecdote Collections and Speaker's Companions

Nigel Rees, author of the *Cassell Dictionary of Anecdotes*, defines an anecdote as "a joke involving actual people." Because people are, according to Stephen Lucas, egocentric and like to hear about things that are meaningful to them (Lucas 1998, 93), anecdotes, themselves stories about people, are an easy way to gain or hold the attention of your audience.

Rees, Nigel. 1999. *The Cassell Dictionary of Anecdotes*. London: Cassell.

This is one of the most enjoyable and useful books of anecdotes I've seen. It is organized by subject (from advice to misapprehensions to zoology) and is extensively indexed by subject, category, and author or quoted speaker. Most anecdotes contain fewer than 100 words, their sources are referenced, and the sources vary from BBC radio programs to *Bartlett's Familiar Quotations*.

Say you've been asked to lead a committee to consider Internet-use policies at your library, with specific atten-

tion given to the growing problem of patrons downloading pornography on public Internet terminals. You could open the meeting with an anecdote:

When Samuel Johnson published his dictionary in 1755, he was loudly praised by two literary ladies for having taken care to omit the naughty words. Dr. Johnson replied, "What, my dears! Then have you been looking for them?" [p. 131].

That happened more than two centuries ago, and now, instead of worrying about naughty words in the dictionary, we worry about the various ways people are using the Internet at our computer stations. Our charge for this committee is to create an Internet-use policy, and yes, that might include a policy regarding pornography, games, and online gambling. I'd like us to start today by listing and discussing the specific issues we may eventually want our policy to address.

I apologize if that sounds a bit like bad movie dialogue. (Now you can see why I never write down my presentations word-for-word.) I offer these examples with the caveat that they're written only to demonstrate the use of the suggested resources, not for their presentation value.

Spinrad, Leonard, and Thelma Spinrad. 1997. *Speaker's Lifetime Library*. Revised and expanded edition Seacaucus, New Jersey: Prentice Hall.

Speaker's companion books can also be useful compendiums of not only anecdotes but also quotes, facts, historical allusions, and other helpful tools to help you be a more interesting speaker, all in one handy source. The second edition of this very handy title combines four volumes in one: the speaker's reference guide, apt comparisons, the day and date book, and the special occasion book. The first section, the speaker's reference guide, is organized by subject (more than 150 of them), and each subject includes definitions, quotations, aphorisms, anecdotes, and facts. The second volume provides a list of common words for which comparisons and symbols, similes and antonyms, and cross-references to other words. The third volume gives a day-by-day account of historical happenings and sample introductions that may be suitable for any occasion on a given day. The last volume provides a sampling of suggested short speeches for a variety of occasions, ranging from making introductions to award acceptance speeches. Although I found the second and fourth volumes less applicable to daily professional life, the first volume of combined quotations and anecdotes and the third section on daily historical allusions were extremely useful as another source of possible introductory, transitional, and concluding attention-grabbers. An example is:

> Popular legend has it that once, when a colleague asked Albert Einstein for his telephone number, Einstein reached for a phone directory and looked it up. The startled man asked, "You don't remember your own phone number?" The great genius shrugged and replied, "Why should I memorize something I can so easily get from a book?" [p. 166].

Books of Quotations

Using quotations to start or conclude a speech (or at any point in between) is one of the most common ways to get your audience to focus on you or to leave them with an idea of the overall theme of your talk. I think part of the appeal is that, quite simply, quotations are fun. They're fun to read, they're fun to repeat (how many forwarded e-mails involving funny or work-related quotes did you receive this week?), and they're fun to listen to. Of all the millions of words and sentences that have been spoken through history, collected quotations are the ones that were funny enough, or thought-provoking enough, or just so universal in appeal that someone took the time to write them down and then repeat them later to make a point or illustrate their own opinions or feelings.

Any number of books of general quotations, as well as an equally great number of very subject-specific quotation books (such as *The Quotable Gardener, The Quotable Cat Lover*) exist for you to consider using or purchasing. For the most part they're also easily obtained; every time I go to a used or library book sale, there's always a copy of *Bartlett's Quotations* or other pocket quotation dictionaries, which brings to mind another positive aspect of using quotations. They never go out of date. Some are more current than others, I'll admit. My 1952 copy of *FPA's Book of Quotations* asserts on the cover that "Everyone knows Franklin P. Adams!" (of the *New Yorker*) which, for all I know, might not have been true even in 1952 (and is less likely now). However, in his section of library-related quotations, he includes an inscription found on a library at Alexandria, Egypt: "A hospital for the mind." Sentiments like that never go out of style.

Andrews, Robert. 1997. *The Cassell Dictionary of Contemporary Quotations*. London: Cassell.

This collection consists entirely of quotations written or uttered after the end of World War II, including but not limited to the works of social commentators, literary critics, comics, songwriters, and screenwriters (from 1,825 different people, in all). The book is organized by subject, for which a table of contents is provided, and extensively indexed by source and key words (a lovely and extremely helpful indexing method).

> A bibliophile of little means is likely to suffer often. Books don't slip from his hands but fly past him through the air, high as birds, high as prices [p. 54].

Frank, Leonard Roy, ed. 1999. *Random House Webster's Quotationary*. New York: Random House.

This "quotationary" contains more than 20,000 quotations (including song lyrics, slogans, and aphorisms) arranged in over 1,000 subject categories, ranging from agriculture to dance to the wise and the foolish. It does not have a subject table of contents but contains a subject category index and a source or author index. Leonard Roy Frank started compiling this work in 1959, based largely on his own reading, which gives it a personal feel and makes its enormity all the more impressive; he has also published two other collections of quotations.

> One question: if this is the Information Age, how come nobody knows anything? [Robert Mankoff, cartoon caption, p. 400].

Miner, Margaret, and Hugh Rawson. 2000. *New International Dictionary of Quotations*. New York: Signet, Putnam.

A steal at $6.99, this little book lives up to its cover claim of including "the best quotations of all time, selected and arranged alphabetically by subject to meet the needs of contemporary readers, writers, and speakers." The editors have previously collaborated on quotation collections from the Bible and from Shakespeare, and admit in their introduction that "its bias, however, is toward the tried and the true," making it a great starter reference, although the editors also state they tried to include more quotes from women and from minority sources, as well as from prose sources (as opposed to poetry). The book is arranged alphabetically by subject and contains an author index that lists the subjects and page numbers on which they are quoted.

> If you can keep your head when all about you / Are losing theirs and blaming it on you. / If you can trust yourself when all men doubt you / And make allowance for their doubting, too [Rudyard Kipling, in *Rewards and Fairies*, 1910, describing virtue].

I found this quote only because the editors included a related quote by Jean Kerr (she's one of my favorite humorists, and it was her name I had looked up) from her book *Please Don't Eat the Daisies*, 1957: "If you can keep your head when all about you are losing theirs, it is just possible that you haven't grasped the situation."

Sound like a quote you could use to describe the first day of any new software implementation?

Torricelli, Robert G., ed. 2001. *Quotations for Public Speakers: A Historical, Literary, and Political Anthology*. New Brunswick, New Jersey: Rutgers University Press.

If a full-time freelance indexer was invited to speak to a library-school indexing class on the realities of self-employment, he might conclude his talk using a quotation:

If you're considering a full-time free-lance career, you have to be realistic about yourself and know your own working style. It's wonderful to set your own schedule, and work for yourself, but you have to be willing to trade the security of a regular paycheck and employer-provided health insurance for long, self-motivated hours and a solitary and sometimes lonely career.

Once you've carefully considered that trade-off, and if you still decide you want to be a freelancer, you're in for a life that won't be ruled by your office — which is one of the reasons I'm still doing it. I firmly believe Robert Frost was right when he said: "The brain is a wonderful organ: it starts working the moment you get up in the morning, and does not stop until you get into the office" [p. 132].

When I started in my first professional librarian position, the only book I took with me to the office was my trusty pocket dictionary of "Quotables from Notables," *The Merriam-Webster Dictionary of Quotations* (Merriam-Webster, Inc., Springfield, Missouri, 1992, cover price $4.99). It has served (and continues to serve) me well, but that doesn't mean I don't still covet all of the other listed quotation books.

Desk References or Companions

Ah, desk references. Sometimes I dream that I'm a librarian in the 1940s, wearing a stylish wool suit (I try not to think about the stockings and heels involved) and horn-rimmed glasses, reaching for my trusty desk reference whenever someone asks what time it is in London or how many pecks there are in a bushel. Today, of course, I just go to convertit.com, or more likely, the patrons stay home and find the information themselves on Yahoo or AskJeeves. Sure, we've gained a little efficiency, but I think we've lost a little style. Nonetheless, desk references offer an amazing array of facts about people, places, events, and things, in a variety of formats including tables, lists, graphs, pictures, and definitions.

Fargis, Paul, ed. 1998. *New York Public Library Desk Reference.* New York: Macmillan.

If this were a perfect world, I would get to spend at least an hour a day just reading this desk reference and learning all it had to teach me; it's my favorite. It consists of more than a thousand glorious pages of facts and information about the physical world, the world of ideas, the way we communicate, daily life, recreation, and the political world. The table of contents is nicely detailed and the index is fifty-five pages long and easy to read, with headings in bold. A speaker might use something like this fact from page 255:

> Isaac Asimov was not only a highly prolific author, he was also extremely versatile. He wrote over four hundred books and is the only author to have a book in every major Dewey decimal category.

Books of Lists

Books of lists will not only help you plan more interesting introductions and conclusions to your presentations, they'll also provide you with a lot of quick and fun reading as well as conversation starters. Not only are there generalized books of lists, but every profession and field of interest seems to have its own book of specialized lists.

Ash, Russell. 1999. *Factastic Book of 1001 Lists.* Buckinghamshire and New York: DK Publishing.

Starting off the bibliography of books of lists by returning to another general collection, one by the author of another great reference work, *The Top Ten of Everything.* This is really a children's nonfiction title, but just because we're adults, we shouldn't lose our appreciation for great information, colorful pictures and illustrations, and the fun of just saying the word, "factastic." True to the title, there's a total of 1001 lists here, ranging in subject from space to people to crime and war and "ultimate lists." Each page is packed with facts, data, names, milestones, definitions, and many other charts and compendia of information. For example, in the section on human achievements, Alice Stebbins Wells is listed as the first-ever policewoman, beginning her career in Los Angeles in 1910 (p. 103). My favorite part of the book is the banner at the top of every page listing a related fact; in the section on language, the banner at the top of the page informs you that there are more than 2,700 languages in the world, and more than 7,000 dialects. The book is complete with an easy-to-read table of contents and index.

Stine, Kate, ed. 1995. *The Armchair Detective Book of Lists: A Complete Guide to the Best Mystery, Crime, and Suspense Fiction.* 2nd ed. New York: Otto Penzler Books.

Edited by the editor of the *Armchair Detective* magazine, this book is a good example of a book of lists that could be useful for a book talk (mysteries account for most libraries' highest circulation numbers) as well as for a personal reference or reading list for someone wishing

to become an expert in the genre. The first part of the book is composed of lists of annual award winners (as named by the Mystery Writers of America and the Crime Writers' Association of Great Britain), while the second part is devoted to lists compiled by mystery critics, famous mystery authors, mystery booksellers, as well as providing a list of mystery organizations, conventions, and publications. For example, Sue Grafton lists among her ten favorite mysteries *Double Indemnity,* by James M. Cain, *The Mysterious Affair at Styles*, by Agatha Christie, and *Talking to Strange Men*, by Ruth Rendell (p. 212).

Wallechinsky, David, and Amy Wallace, eds. 1993. *The Book of Lists: The 90s Edition.* Boston and New York: Little, Brown and Company.

Compiled by the same people who produce the annual *People's Almanac,* this book is one of my favorites. Don't be discouraged by the 1993 publication date; many of the lists included involve historical and trivial content that goes out of date less quickly than do other reference books that depend more heavily on recent facts and numbers. The book includes sections on people, movies and TV, the arts, health and food, animals, work, family and relationships, crime, politics and world affairs, America, travel, literature, words, advice, sports, and, of course, miscellany. Many of the lists themselves are contributed by experts in those fields and other recognized authorities; here you'll find Joyce Carol Oates's fourteen favorite American authors (interesting information to include if you're giving a book talk that includes titles written by Oates) and Dr. Andrew Weil's list of eleven common medical procedures that he would recommend avoiding.

Thirty-three famous people who suffer or suffered from diabetes are listed, including Arthur Ashe, Miles Davis, Thomas Edison, Ernest Hemingway, and Mary Tyler Moore (p. 119).

That information, as well as the introductory paragraph that lists many of the early symptoms of the disease, could be an interesting way to introduce a public library program that features a health speaker, or to any information professional who works in a health-related special library.

Almanacs

Almanacs remain one of the few reference books that can still provide me with answers to certain questions faster than the Internet can. For specific information about U.S. states (bird, emblem, area) in particular, a good up-to-date almanac presents the most credible and cleanly organized data possible. What many people don't know is that many almanacs also provide minibiographies on the presidents, chronologies of history, fascinating crime data, and business and technology statistics.

Next to quotations, statistics are one of the most commonly used attention-getters, and all almanacs are as long on statistics and facts, as they are short on superfluous information. Of course, unlike quotation collections, almanacs can and do go out of date. Although older almanacs can be useful for the data and yearly summaries, for the latest data and most current statistics, you will need to obtain the most recent almanac. A public librarian giving a talk on travel resources might open with a fact obtained from:

Robert Famighetti's *The 2000 World Almanac and Book of Facts* (Mahwah, New Jersey: Primedia Reference).

In 1998, the average number of vacation days an Italian took was forty-two. If you were French, you got thirty-seven, and if you were German, your average number of vacation days was thirty-five. Contrast that with the average of thirteen days for Americans, and you'll see that carefully planning your vacation is necessary to fit everything into those thirteen days that you possibly can. Today we'll be looking at a few of this year's hottest destinations, the best guidebooks available, and the newest travel websites that exist to help you book your trip at the cheapest rates possible.

Wallechinsky, David. 1995. *The 20th Century: The Definitive Compendium of Astonishing Events, Amazing People, and Strange-but-True Facts.* New York and Boston: Little, Brown and Company.

I recently spent a lovely Saturday night reading through this book of twentieth-century facts and events, and felt quite smug the entire next week about knowing the details of the Sacco and Vanzetti case from 1920, the fact that the microwave was invented in 1945, and how "Merkle's Boner" helped the New York Giants lose the 1912 World Series. The book begins with a short "quote-book" from the twentieth century on a variety of subjects, and progresses through chapters on the high and the mighty, disasters, crime, war, animals, travel and transportation, sky and space, communication, movies, television, arts and performers, news, science and technology, health, family and leisure, sports, religion, death, and strange stories. It is also well-indexed, by name and subject.

The Committee on Public Doublespeak of the National Council of Teachers of English began giving Doublespeak awards in 1974. The awards are a "tribute" to public figures who use language that is "grossly deceptive, evasive, euphemistic, confusing, or self-contradictory" [p. 393].

The 1984 award went to the U.S. Department of State, which announced that the word *killing* would no longer be used in its annual reports on human rights around the world. Instead, *killing* would be replaced with the phrase "unlawful or arbitrary deprivation of life" [p. 395].

A number of specialized almanacs exist, such as the *People's Sports Almanac*, the *American Political Almanac*, and so on. Take a look through some of the more recent almanacs at the public library or any bookstore to get a feel for their contents and organization, to see which one might be most helpful to your specific area of expertise, as well as one that you find logically organized and well-indexed.

Wright, John W., ed. 2001. The New York Times *Almanac 2002*. New York: Penguin USA.

This almanac not only provides short pieces from the pages of the *New York Times*, but delivers all that an almanac should, organized into six sections covering events of the year, the United States, the world, science and technology, awards and prizes, and sports. It also includes a comprehensive index and several pages of detailed maps. At a cover price of $10.95 for paperback, it combines value with an unbeatable source for facts.

In 1990, 46,748 new editions and new books were published; by 1999, that number was 119,357 [p. 394].

Librariana

Books of facts, quotations, or cartoons about librarians and librarianship can be extremely useful resources. A large number of speaking opportunities in our profession are speaking among and to one another, and part of knowing your audience is using information or attention-getters that are tailored especially for them. A group of undergraduate students would not understand most of the library cartoons out there, but your fellow librarians will, and it is foolish not to avail yourself of the humor and resources that have been created for you by your professional colleagues.

Eberhart, George M. 2000. *The Whole Library Handbook 3*. Chicago: American Library Association.

In the introduction I quoted Mary Jane Scherdin's article on librarians and their personality types as described by the Myers-Briggs Personality Indicator, which is information I never would have found were it not for this book. It's a very handy library reference book on libraries, including data and curiosa from all aspects of librarianship, from people, materials, and guidelines, to funding, diversity, and staff development. The compiler points out one of my favorite aspects of handbooks when searching for the perfect information to include in your presentation: "A handbook is quicker to browse for serendipitous discoveries than surfing the web. The feel of one's thumb flipping through physical pages is also more satisfying and natural than link hopping or exploring Yahoo" (Eberhart 2000, v). The very first article in the book, "Some Basic Figures," by Mary Jo Lynch (and the ALA Office for Research and Statistics), should indicate the depth of what this book has to offer:

The 1996 NCES (National Center for Education Statistics) report on public libraries shows 1,013,798,000 "visits" in that year, an increase of 3.2% over the figure in the 1995 report. In 1996, the average circulation for public libraries was 6.5 items per capita. The total number of items circulated nationally from public libraries in 1996 was over 1,642,625,000, an increase of 2% more than the figure reported in 1995 [p. 3].

Things like that may be useful to know and be able to quote, especially in times of budget shortfalls and at local government meetings when the worth of the library is questioned.

Epstein, Benita L. 1998. *Interlibrary Loan Sharks and Seedy Roms: Cartoons from Libraryland*. Jefferson, North Carolina: McFarland & Company.

This book is divided into four parts ("Inside the Library," "Outside the Library," "Technology," and "Writers, Scholars, and Artists"), and you're sure to find a cartoon that's applicable to any meeting or presentation situation. I particularly like this book because many other sources use words rather than images, and because cartoons offer people who do not feel comfortable telling jokes or humorous anecdotes a way to comfortably use humor.

Harding, Les. 1994. *A Book in Hand Is Worth Two in the Library: Quotations on Books and Librarianship*. Jefferson, North Carolina: McFarland & Company.

Books about libraries also come in such helpful and specialized forms as quotation books. This is a great quotation collection, organized into ten chapters covering library topics such as li-brarians, borrowing and lending, classics, and education. It's very easy to use because of its extensive indexing, both by speaker or writer and by subject and key word, and pleasant to read straight through, thanks to its short prose explanations and transitions between quotations. Last but not least, the author even concludes his preface with a Blaise Pascal quotation: "Let it not be said that I have said nothing new. The arrangement of the material is new" (Harding 1994, 5). What circulation librarian hasn't dreamed of securing a warning to all books like the threat used by Pope Nicholas V: "Whoever writes his name here in acknowledgment of books received on loan out of the Pope's Library, will incur his anger and his curse unless he return them uninjured within a very brief period" (Harding 1994, 63.)

Manley, Will. 1994. *Uncensored Thoughts: Pot Shots from a Public Librarian*. Jefferson, North Carolina: McFarland & Company.

The official book of anecdotes for all things librarian (public and otherwise), this is a highly enjoyable book that should yield any number of stories, as told by Will Manley, that could be used for any presentation by librarians, to librarians. There are no chapters here, only titles such as "Librarians and Food" and "Garbage In, Garbage Out" to break up the text. There is a table of contents, squashed between the acknowledgments and the preface on page twelve, and there is an index, but it is so short and obviously not meant to be used that it can't be. It's still worth the time to give the book a read and mark favorite stories or appropriate anecdotes for future reference, and I can forgive the lack of a proper index for the author's admission that he originally wanted to call the book *Uncivil Liberties*. He relented when a friend pointed out that Calvin Trillin had already written a book under that title, and suggested that he reconsider using it because "Calvin Trillin has more brains in his elbow than you have in your head."

The fact is that the prophets of doom have a terrible track record with the book. They've had it dead, buried, and forgotten too many times to count over the past 125 years and, like a stubborn cockroach, it keeps reappearing strong and healthier than ever in the face of new and more powerful technologies. Thomas Edison of all people began the funeral obsequies for the book in 1878 when, shortly after unveiling his first fragile phonograph, he boldly predicted that his new talking machine would supplant the printing press as a transmitter of culture [p. 130].

Trivia Books and Websites

Considering what books and reference sources on general bits of trivia and "fun facts" I've used or would like to consult for future presentations has been, by far, the most entertaining part of creating this book. I've enjoyed it so much that it's actually been bad for my productivity; why suggest different titles and ways to reference them when they're sitting, tantalizingly, on my desk, just waiting to be read? Last week I learned that cat urine is ultra-concentrated because cats were originally desert animals and retain characteristics of that desert physiology (Thomas 2001) and because I own a cat and know others who own cats, I've already gotten to share that detail twice. You may ask what that has to do with public speaking, and you may

dislike cats, so I hope I haven't lost you before I get to this suggestion: if you're stumped on how to start, conclude, or spice up a presentation, buy or check out one of the hundreds of available "fun fact," "trivia quiz," or "question and answer" books that are available on any subject or subjects you can imagine. Often they have very helpful indexes that should suggest thematic ways to begin or conclude your talk, and even if you don't find information you can use, it's never a bad idea to step back from your presentation, read or do something else, and then return to it refreshed. The books and sources listed below are the most refreshing and helpful that I've used and enjoyed.

McLain, Bill. 2001. *What Makes Flamingos Pink? A Colorful Collection of Q & A's for the Unquenchably Curious.* New York: HarperCollins. (Also see McLain, Bill. 1999. *Do Fish Drink Water? Puzzling and Improbable Questions and Answers. New York: Morrow.*)

Bill McClain's official title is webmaster for Xerox, and while fulfilling his responsibility for handling all of the e-mail that individuals send to the company's website, he found that many of the questions he was receiving had nothing to do with Xerox, or even technology. These two titles are a compendium of the questions he's received and answered, and range in subject matter from the animal kingdom, to language, to science, and back to "off the wall." Each chapter is organized by subject and then divided by question, after which follows the answer, a number of factoids, and a section of further related information under the heading "Did You Know?" Both books include tables of contents including all of the questions, as well as subject indexes, making them vastly more valuable than the great number of similar books (such as *Just Curious, Jeeves: What Are the 1001 Most Intriguing Questions Asked on the Internet?*, Jack Mingo and Erin Barrett, AskJeeves, Emeryville, CA, 2000) that have handicapped themselves by not providing an index.

A speaker might say something like this:

> The original question was "Why do your palms sweat when you are nervous?" Part of the answer, at least, is that "the majority of the roughly five million sweat glands in your body are concentrated on the palms of your hands, the soles of your feet, and, to some extent, your armpits. About two-thirds of the glands are in your hands … if you are in a stressful situation and are nervous, angry, embarrassed, or anxious, your entire nervous system reacts and produces an immediate response called 'flight or fight….' This type of emotionally induced sweating is limited to your hands, feet, and armpits." In the Did You Know? section related to this question, the author also relates that humans often do not have conscious control over their body language, which some authorities claim accounts for ninety-three percent of our communication with others [from McLain 2001, 125].

When would you share information like that in a library setting? Perhaps if you were asked to be a panel member at a library school's colloquium on gaining employment in the library profession, or if you were offering a workshop on better professional communication techniques. Those random bits of information, for as long as you can remember them, anyway, can also be used in daily conversation. Remember the tip in

Chapter 11 about putting a candy dish your desk so people would make it a point to stop or congregate and talk by your desk? Having something to say other than comments on the weather might also help you be more relaxed in your interactions with others, and that's always beneficial. I'll admit you may not want to jump right in with the information about cats and their desert physiology, but I promise you that knowing that the oldest living thing in the world is considered to be the 12,000-year-old creosote bush in California's Mohave Desert isn't going to make you a duller person.

Useless Knowledge, www.uselessknowl edge.com

The Useless Knowledge website has proven infinitely valuable to me during past presentations, and I still refer to it on a weekly basis whenever I need a good, old-fashioned, truly random fact. Not only can you ask the site to randomly generate facts for you, but you can also search its database of over 25,000 facts, as well as browse its quotation collection and learn a new "word of the day." For example, you might learn:

> Aristotle, Sir Isaac Newton, and Charles Darwin had a problem expressing themselves because they stuttered.

Subject Specialty Trivia Books

In addition to general trivia and nonfiction collections, you may also know of a number of fine resources in your subject area. Law, history, science, and literature are represented by the following resources, respectively. These sources (in these subject areas) are the ones I've had the good fortune to use. Rest assured, however, that regardless of your subject specialty, you should be able to find reference works similar to those I've listed.

The Engines of Our Ingenuity, www.uh. edu/engines/

I haven't worked in the engineering library for years, but this site remains near the top of my bookmark list. The Engines of Our Ingenuity is a radio program written and hosted by John Lienhard, the M.D. Anderson Professor of Mechanical Engineering and History at the University of Houston. I often referred to the site's more than 1,700 program transcripts when I wanted to be inspired by its homage to human creativity as embodied in technological and scientific advances. For example:

> Were you aware that gear teeth are far more than just wedges protruding from a wheel — that their shapes have been mathematically contrived so that smooth, almost-flat surfaces push against one another without any sliding? Furthermore, gears are designed so the back of each tooth very nearly stays in contact with the mating tooth. That way the gear can be reversed without backlash. Some very complex human ingenuity has been used to avoid the sharp edges, sliding motion, and backlash that wear gears out [http://www.uh.edu/engines/epi49.htm].

Glossbrenner, Alfred, and Emily Glossbrenner. 2000. *About the Author*. San Diego, New York, and London: Cader Books, Harcourt Inc.

Nothing's more exciting than starting or finishing a book talk or a book group with suggestions for further or related readings, or with information on how authors can be contacted. This book provides both brief biographical facts

and longer explanations of more than 125 authors' writing styles and influences. It also provides an overview of the authors' own works, as well as suggested references for further research and works of criticism (under the heading "Treatises and Treats").

Richardson, Matthew. 1997. *Whose Bright Idea Was That? Great Firsts of World History*. New York: Kodansa America.

This book merits inclusion under the subject of "history" primarily because the word appears in the title; it could just as easily have been placed under "science" or "law" or "business." The author has sought to provide the most accurate account of the world's true firsts, as well as starting the book with a chart of commonly claimed (but inaccurate) firsts, including the suggestions that golf was not invented by the Scots, and that Sigmund Freud was not the first person to theorize about the human subconscious. Any librarian wishing to give a presentation on local legal resources and searching might be interested to learn and pass along the information that the first laws prohibiting noise-producing activities were passed in the Greek city of Sybaris (in southwest Italy) in the sixth century B.C. (p. 375). This book is a true librarian's delight: in the back you'll find not only a comprehensive index but also a chronological table of entries, so you can search the book by subject and time period.

Schwartz, Bernard. 1997. *A Book of Legal Lists: The Best and Worst in American Law*. Oxford and New York: Oxford University Press.

Bernard Schwartz has written a number of books on the Supreme Court and is responsible for compiling this first collection of American legal bests and worsts. The lists vary from the Ten Greatest Supreme Court Justices to the Ten Greatest Legal Motion Pictures, each with substantive explanations and history. The lists are the personal opinion of the author, who states in the preface that they are based on over half a century's experience in the law. All of them are interesting to read and among those in the legal professions (including law librarians) are sure to foster discussion. The book also includes more than one hundred trivia questions on the Supreme Court, the chief justices, presidents and the Court, and the greatest Supreme Court judges. A speaker might use something like this:

> The issue of the legal right of privacy is not a new one. According to trivia question twenty-four, Justice Louis D. Brandeis (himself #6 on the list of the ten greatest Supreme Court justices) originated the right in his 1890 article, "The Right to Privacy" [p. 275].

Tuleja, Tad. 1992. *American History in 100 Nutshells*. New York: Fawcett Columbine.

How could I not recommend a book that promises to "help you win friends, influence national policy, and appear savvier on our great democratic experiment than the professor who gave you a B minus in AmHist 101 could have imagined"? Presented here you'll find 100 of the most commonly heard and least understood quotes and phrases from American history, from "Go West, young man" to short explanations of the Wisconsin Idea and the Gilded Age, complete with factual tidbits at the end of each section and concluded with a comprehensive index. For any academic librarian wishing to impress a group of undergraduates wondering how to find the shortest possible synopses of American history, this is the book to quote from and suggest. Also by Tad Tuleja: *Fabulous Fallacies, Beyond the Bottom Line, Curious Customs, Marvelous Monikers, Foreignisms, The Cat's Pajamas, The Catalog of Lost Books,* and *Quirky Quotations*.

Absolutely Last, but Not Least

Although you may never produce your own book of quotations like Leonard Frank Roy did, now is the best time to begin your very own tickler file of things that you read or hear that just strike you as funny, true, shocking, or just plain catchy. You never know when one of them may turn out to be useful; the Patrick McManus quote at the beginning of this chapter comes from my very own tickler file, which has served me well through a number of presentations. I started my file several years ago, with something I heard on The *Simpsons*. I'm glad I did, because it feels like the perfect quote to leave you with.

> *If I could say a few words ... I'd be a better public speaker!*
> — Homer Simpson

APPENDIX 3

Presentation Software Tips

As librarians and library professionals, we work in an environment of constantly changing technologies and user interfaces, as well as software packages that require frequent updating and training. The research literature of our field is littered with demands that we change our image and our competencies to become more focused on technical skills; to adapt ourselves to a library world that centers less on a physical facility or traditional print tools than it does on remote learning, advanced database design and programming, and web and software production skills.

Research also shows that we ourselves are not immune to the visual presentation's charms. A 1998 study of seventy-four Chicago librarians concluded that "when comparing the oral and web-based visual presentation with an oral presentation and handouts, respondents strongly supported the effectiveness of the former over the latter. Seventy-two percent agreed or strongly agreed that the oral and web-based presentation organized information better, and fifty percent agreed or strongly agreed that the flow of the oral and web-based visual presentation was smoother" (Casey 2000, 14). In such an environment, it's easy to get carried away with a desire to wow our audiences, not with our speaking skills or our command of the topic, but rather with a slick production in the form of presentation or Internet "slides," complete with animated bullet points and professional graphics.

This entire appendix will be devoted to tips and hints for designing the best possible such presentation, but before we approach those tips, I have to display my own technophobe and reactionary roots and offer one small caveat: No software presentation, no matter how well-designed or professionally produced, is a substitute for a skilled and adaptable speaker who makes every effort to connect with his or her audience and who commands knowledge of and enthusiasm for the topic. Just as we have all sat through boring or unprepared presentations by poor speakers, we have all also been subjected to software presentations crowded with whistles, bells, animations, graphics ... and very little interesting or useful information. This appendix will not offer specific tips for any one software or Internet graphics package; any number of manuals and *For Dummies* titles exist to help you master whatever specific programs you will work with privately or at your institution. What follows are broad suggestions, culled from presentation skills manuals, research articles, and my own experience.

Tip #1: Ask yourself: do you really need to prepare an online or software presentation?

The first step to effectively using presentation software is to know when not to use it. Designing and using electronic presentations, just like using transparent overheads or any other kind of visual aid, automatically adds to your preparation time and introduces another way in which problems can arise during your presentation (such as your particular presentation not working on another computer, no computer being available where you're speaking, having problems connecting to the live Internet; the possibilities for error are varied and endless). Although using presentation software can allow you to connect with audience members who have more visual learning styles, or who simply expect you to use every new software package because it's there to be used, there are a few situations in which you may find it vastly advantageous not to fuss with an electronic presentation:

✓ You expect your presentation to last fewer than fifteen minutes.

✓ Your presentation contains very little technical or specific information.

✓ Your speech is designed more for emotional appeal than for information dissemination.

✓ You are not demonstrating or discussing any specific database, product, or Internet connection.

✓ You have limited time in which to prepare your speech.

✓ You anticipate that your speaking environment will be informal (such as at a small department meeting, or when meeting with one or a small group of students).

✓ Your audience will consist of people who might have difficulty seeing or understanding your slides (the elderly, people with different levels of language skills).

✓ The purpose of your speech is to introduce, emcee, or to facilitate any event or discussion.

Tip #2: Plan your preparation time realistically.

As anyone who has ever spent time playing around with Adobe PhotoShop, Microsoft PowerPoint, or even Microsoft Word can tell you, time flies when you're learning and using graphics and presentation or layout software. Although you should approach creating your electronic presentation only after your speech outline has been written and practiced, using software or the Internet to create slides is not something you can leave until the last minute. If you estimate that it will take you about two hours to create some basic outline slides, you'll most likely find that it takes you in excess of four or more hours, not counting initial brainstorming and sketching-on-paper time, or time afterward to proofread your handiwork. A good, conservative plan is to double the longest amount of time that you would guess you could possibly spend creating your online or electronic presentation. If you are a person who dislikes or has difficulty working with new software packages, or feel limited in your ability to work with layout and graphics, quadruple your time.

Tip #3: Write or sketch out all of your slides or webpages before using the software.

Find some scrap paper, consult your speech outline or notes, and list or draw the main points, information, and graphics you'd like to include in your electronic presentation. That is advantageous for two reasons: it will allow you to get a feel for the big picture of your topic (which will help you remain consistent among slides or pages) rather than becoming instantly mired down in the aesthetic details of individual slides; and, if you become disenchanted with the look or flow of your slides on paper, it's much easier to throw them away and start over than it will be once you start using the software. Trust me, after you've invested a few hours in picking colors, fonts, clip art, and animated bullets, you're not going to have the heart to ditch a poorly conceived slide show, no matter how much of a disservice it will do you during the actual presentation. Your scrap-paper drawings and storyboards don't have to be fancy or well-drawn; they'll exist only long enough to give you a feel for the scope of your presentation, and to give you a starting place when you begin working with the presentation or web software of your choice.

Tip #4: Keep your slides or webpages short, and use concise language.

Most of the literature available on this subject advises using four or fewer bullet points per slide, and seven or fewer words per sentence. Although your listeners can hear more words per minute than you can say, their ability to listen carefully decreases with every visual piece of information that you present to them. Presenting less information per slide also gives you the option to use larger type sizes (for easier reading) and more powerful use of graphic "white space." Although one of the main advantages of presenting a slide or Internet demonstration is the ability it gives you to relate to more visual learners, never forget that your slides exist to supplement you and your presentation, not the other way around. Likewise, using concise language is important for all of the same reasons that it was during your speaking: the simpler and clearer your words and sentences, the better chance you stand of being understood by everyone in your audience, regardless of gender, language, age, or any other demographic factors.

In addition to keeping individual slides short and your language concise, experts further advise that you "don't use too many screens, since it takes thirty to forty-five seconds for the audience to absorb the information on each, and you really want them to look at you rather than at the screen! So have no more than one visual every two or three minutes" (Weaver 1999, 64).

Tip #5: Be consistent.

Consistency has gotten a bad rap for being the hobgoblin of little minds, but if your audience has to adjust to each slide's new color scheme, type size or font, or animations, they'll have less time to read and comprehend the information you provide, and even less time to concentrate on what you're saying at the same time. Contrary to popular belief, consistency among slides in the areas of text justification, color schemes, and language doesn't make for a boring presentation; depending on dynamic software bells and whistles does. You need look no further than pop culture for proof of this phenomenon; read any number of film reviews of *Star Wars II: Attack of the Clones*, and you'll find that most fault the film's dependence on visual effects at the expense of its story and dialogue.

Tip #6: Learn a little something about layout and design.

Just as reading about various communication theories and techniques will help you improve your own speaking and presentational style, reading about the successful elements of graphics and layout design will help you create the most useful visual presentations. It shouldn't take very long to find or consult any resource for this kind of information; any number of manuals, journal articles, or freely available Internet guides are available on the subject and offer small but significant pieces of purely aesthetic advice such as:

✓ Serif typefaces (like the one you're reading now) are easier to read, but sans serif typefaces such as arial stand up well to projection and are bolder in appearance (Rabb 1993, 83).

✓ There's no need to be a slave to exact numbers; audiences will better understand and remember approximate and round numbers than lengthy decimals or odd numbers (Rabb 1993, 14).

✓ Clip art can add interest to your slides, and most presentation software packages offer some sort of basic clip art library, which you can use without worrying about copyright (Lowe 2001, 130).

✓ Keep your slide or screen background simple; the purpose of the background is to provide a well-defined visual space for the slide's content (Lowe 2001, 305).

Tip #7: Cite your information sources.

Nothing is more frustrating for audience members than having to wonder where a presenter found the information, quotes, statistics, charts, photographs, or other sources that he or she considered important enough to highlight in an electronic presentation. That should be a no-brainer for librarians, the gatekeepers of copyright and citation issues, but all too often source citations are omitted because the person creating the graphics simply ran out of time to provide the documentation, or deemed that a citation unnecessarily cluttered up a slide or webpage. You don't need to make it the most prominent piece of information on the page, but you do have to make sure it's there. It's important for your own peace of mind (what if someone asks where a certain piece of information came from?), it's important for copyright, and it's important for establishing your credibility with the audience. Credibility is one of the most important factors determining how much your audience will listen to you, so always cite your sources, on your visuals and during your presentation.

Tip #8: Proofread and practice your electronic presentation carefully.

Nothing destroys speaker credibility faster than typos, poor grammar, or just plain misinformation on your visual aids, slides, or Internet pages. Overlooking such purely image-related details is unforgivable in this age of software spell- and grammar-checkers. Practice speaking along with your slide presentation early and often; not only will repeated practices help you spot inconsistencies as well as grammatical errors, but it will also help you become proficient with juggling your speaking notes and the keyboard or other tools you'll be using. If you are too tired of your presentation topic after preparing it to give it the proofreading attention it needs, ask a colleague or friend to look it over for you (after offering to return the favor at any time, of course), so they can spot any typos or errors you may have missed.

Further Reading

All Good Things Typography, www.redsun. com/type/. A very nice online guide for choosing and using the best typefaces, as well as a glossary, history of type, and rules for combining type and graphics for the best results in your documents. The page also includes links to various font download pages and libraries.

Holmes, Nigel, *Designer's Guide to Creating Charts and Diagrams*, New York, Watson-Guptill Publications, 1984. Yes, it's old, but it is, hands down, the best resource I've ever seen for succinctly defining the various types of charts and graphs any presenter could create for a web- or software-based presentation slide show, as well as for offering strict suggestions for when each type might be used to its full advantage (for example: pie charts are best used for showing up to eight or ten component parts of a whole, such as budgets, share of market figures, or analysis of income and spending (Holmes 1984, 25). In addition to definitions and suggestions for use, the book is full of examples of charts and tables, many of which are quite colorful, and all of which are quite creative (such as the stacks of coins used to show casinos' net earnings in a bar graph). At the time of the book's publication, Nigel Holmes was the deputy art director for *Time* magazine, and many of the fantastic examples given are from that publication.

Joss, Molly W., *Looking Good in Presentations*, 3rd edition, Albany NY, Coriolis Group, 1999. A straightforward and compelling look at how best to create and use electronic presentations, either in addition to your speeches or as stand-alone products. Chapters outlining the importance of careful planning are followed by chapters on the specifics of good design principles and graphics consideration. The final chapters explore the use of web-based presentations, sample scenarios and layouts, and tips for refining and proofreading prepared presentations. A lengthy resource guide at the end of the book includes addresses and URLs for companies that sell presentation software packages, web-based presentation and graphics tools, and computer hardware and presentation equipment.

Kentie, Peter, *Web Design: Tools and Techniques*, 2nd edition, Berkeley, CA, Peachpit Press, 2002. Because presenters often create websites or web slides specifically for presentations, knowing some of the basic principles of good web design can't hurt (especially if your library duties happen to include web design or editing as well as public speaking). This book jumps right in by providing ten basic rules for good design, from first picking up a pencil to sketch out the webpage structure, to using common sense technology and designing with restraint because most users still want to see information on the page quickly, in less than ten seconds. More detailed chapters offer advice on the best colors, backgrounds, text, and tables and frames to use when designing webpages or slides for maximum usability. Much of the book is too advanced and specific to be used for generic design principles, but if you can check out a copy from your own library or one nearby, it's well worth a quick and informative scan, and includes a specific and nicely formatted index (indented, which is easier to read and use than run-in) that can take you to whatever information you need quickly.

Lowe, Doug, *PowerPoint 2002 for Dummies*, Hungry Minds, New York, 2001. No matter which presentation or Internet page creation software package you choose to use, there's most likely a *For Dummies* title available to help you learn how best to use it. Overcome your righteous indignation at being called a dummy (if you could see how often I've checked *Sex for Dummies* out to patrons, you'd realize there's no reason to hang on to your pride regarding these books) and consult one; when you've got quick questions about which menu is hiding the command you need to add a shadow to your clip art, these are the books that can answer those questions for you, complete with handy illustrations and screen captures telling you where to click. These books are hugely successful because they make software programs (and other things) more accessible, and because they're written to be understood with as little effort and as small a time investment as possible.

Rabb, Margaret Y., *The Presentation Design Book: Tips, Techniques, and Advice for Creating Effective, Attractive Slides, Overheads, Screen Shows, Multimedia, and More*, Chapel Hill, North Carolina, Ventana Press, 1993. A fantastic resource for all things design, this book is an easy and quick read. Chapters 4 and 5 are particularly useful their emphasis on design and layout principles regarding text, colors, and content placement; and chapter 11 on commonly made novice mistakes is also enlightening. The quickest ways to achieve different effects and results are offered in a straightforward style, and the book includes a comprehensive index that makes it easy to delve into with the most specific of questions and concerns.

Bibliography

An asterisk (*) indicates an item of interest not cited in the text.

*Aguilar, Leslie, and Linda Stokes. 1996. *Multicultural Customer Service: Providing Outstanding Service Across Cultures.* Burr Ridge, Illinois: Irwin Professional Publishing.

Andrews, Robert. 1997. *The Cassell Dictionary of Contemporary Quotations.* London: Cassell.

Antonelli, Monika, Jeff Kempe, and Greg Sidberry. 2000. And Now for Something Completely Different.... Theatrical Techniques for Library Instruction. *Research Strategies* 17:177–185.

Aristotle. 1954. *Aristotle's Rhetoric and Poetics.* Translated by W. R. Roberts and I. Bywater. New York: Modern Library, Random House.

Ash, Russell. 1999. *Factastic Book of 1001 Lists.* Buckinghamshire and New York: DK Publishing.

Avery, Elizabeth Fuseler, Terry Dahlin, and Deborah A. Carver, eds. 2001. *Staff Development: A Practical Guide.* 3rd ed. Chicago and London: American Library Association.

Barclay, Donald A., ed. 1995. *Teaching Electronic Information Literacy: A How-To-Do-It Manual, How-To-Do-It Manuals for Librarians, Number 53.* New York and London: Neal-Schuman Publishers, Inc.

Barzun, Jacques. 1991. *Begin Here: The Forgotten Conditions of Teaching and Learning.* Chicago and London: University of Chicago Press.

Baxter, Kathleen. 1998. Booktalking Basics. *School Library Journal* 44 (6):70–71.

Berra, Yogi. 1999. *I Really Didn't Say Everything I Said!* New York: Workman Publishing.

Bertot, John Carlo, and Charles R. McClure. 2000. Public Libraries and the Internet 2000: Summary Findings and Data Tables. Washington D.C.: National Commission on Libraries and Information Science.

Bienvenu, Sherron. 2000. *The Presentation Skills Workshop: Helping People Create and Deliver Great Presentations.* New York: AMACOM.

Blass, Thomas. *The Stanley Milgram Website* [cited 23 June 2002]. Available from http://www.stanleymilgram.com/.

Bridges, Karl. 2001. Why Traditional Librarianship Matters. *American Libraries* 32 (10):52–54.

Brinkman, Rick, and Rick Kirschner. 1994. *Dealing with People You Can't Stand: How to Bring Out the Best in People at Their Worst.* New York: McGraw-Hill, Inc.

Brody, Marjorie. 1998. Delivering Your Speech Right Between Their Eyes. *American Salesman* 43 (8):29–30.

Burley-Allen, Madelyn. 1995. *Listening: The Forgotten Skill.* 2nd ed. New York: John Wiley and Sons.

153

_____. 2001. Listen Up. *HRMagazine* 46 (11):115–120.

Burnett, Carol. 1986. *One More Time*. New York: Random House.

Camp, Richaurd, May E. Vielhaber, and Jack L. Simonetti. 2001. *Strategic Interviewing: How to Hire Good People, University of Michigan Business School Management Series*. San Francisco: Jossey-Bass.

Casey, Diane Dates. 2000. Oral and Web-based Visual Presentations: 21st Century Professional Development for Librarians and Library Staff. *Illinois Libraries* 82 (1):12–18.

Clark, Alice S., and Kay F. Jones, eds. 1986. *Teaching Librarians to Teach: On-the-Job Training for Bibliographic Instruction Librarians*. Metuchen, NJ: Scarecrow Press.

Coffman, Steve, and Susan McGlamery. 2000. The Librarian and Mr. Jeeves. *American Libraries* 31 (5):66–69.

Conroy, Barbara, and Barbara Schindler Jones. 1986. *Improving Communication in the Library*. Phoenix, Arizona: The Oryx Press.

*Cottringer, William, and Lora Haberer. 2001. Power Communication. *Executive Excellence* 18 (4):15.

Crowley, B. 1996. Redefining the Status of the Librarian in Higher Education. *College and Research Libraries* 48:113–121.

Dale, Paulette, Ph.D. 1999. "*Did You Say Something, Susan?" How Any Woman Can Gain Confidence with Assertive Communication*. Secaucus, New Jersey: Birch Lane Press, Carol Publishing Group.

Day, Ruth S. 1980. Teaching from Notes: Some Cognitive Consequences. *New Directions for Teaching and Learning* 2:95–111.

DeVito, Joseph A. 1976. *The Interpersonal Communication Book*. New York: Harper & Row.

*_____, and M.L. Hecht, eds. 1990. *The Nonverbal Communication Reader*. Prospect Heights, Illinois: Waveland Press.

Dewey, Barbara I., and Sheila D. Creth. 1993. *Team Power: Making Library Meetings Work*. Chicago and London: American Library Association.

Dimitrius, Jo-Ellan, and Mark Mazzarella. 1998. *Reading People*. New York: Ballantine Books.

Drucker, Doris. 2000. How Not to Mumble. *Training & Development* 54 (2):71–72.

Eberhart, George M. 2000. *The Whole Library Handbook 3*. Chicago: American Library Association.

Edwards, Paul N. *How to Give a Talk: Changing the Culture of Academic Public Speaking* [cited 15 June 2002]. Available from http://www.si.umich.edu/~pne/acadtalk.htm.

Ekman, Paul, and Richard J. Davidson. 1993. Voluntary Smiling Changes Regional Brain Activity. *Psychological Science* 4 (5):342–345.

Epstein, Benita L. 1998. *Interlibrary Loan Sharks and Seedy Roms: Cartoons from Libraryland*. Jefferson, North Carolina: McFarland & Company.

Eye Contact: The Over-looked Presentation Tool. 1998. *Sales & Marketing Management* 150 (13):80.

Famighetti, Robert, ed. 1999. *The 2000 World Almanac and Book of Facts*. Mahwah, New Jersey: Primedia Reference.

Fargis, Paul, ed. 1998. *New York Public Library Desk Reference*. New York: Macmillan.

Fatt, James P.T. 1999. It's Not What You Say, It's How You Say It. *Communication World* 16 (6):37–40.

Frank, Leonard Roy, ed. 1999. *Random House Webster's Quotationary*. New York: Random House.

*Freeman, Lisa. 2000. What Makes for a Good 1st Impression? Some Surprises. *Credit Union Journal* 4 (28):5–6.

Frost, Joyce Hocker, and William W. Wilmot. 1978. *Interpersonal Conflict*. Dubuque, Iowa: William C. Brown Company, Publishers.

*Fry, Ron. 2000. *Ask the Right Questions, Hire the Best People*. Franklin Lakes, New Jersey: The Career Press, Inc.

Giesecke, Joan, ed. 1992. *Practical Help for New Supervisors*. Chicago and London: American Library Association.

Glickstein, Lee. 1998. *Be Heard Now!* New York: Bantam Doubleday Dell.

*Glossbrenner, Alfred, and Emily Glossbrenner. 2000. *About the Author*. San Diego, New York, and London: Cader Books, Harcourt Inc.

Goldstein, Sharon, ed. 1992. *The Merriam-Webster Dictionary of Quotations*. Springfield, Massachusetts: Merriam-Webster, Inc.

Goodman, Gary S. 2000. *Please Don't Shoot the Messenger: How to Talk to Demanding Bosses, Clueless Colleagues, Tough Customers, and Difficult Clients Without Losing Your Cool (Or Your Job!)*. Chicago, Illinois: Contemporary Books.

*Gordon, Rachel Singer. 2001. *Teaching the Internet in Libraries*. Chicago and London: American Library Association.

*Gottesman, Deb, and Buzz Mauro. 1999. *The Interview Rehearsal Book: 7 Steps to Job-winning Interviews Using Acting Skills You Never Knew You Had*. New York: Berkley Books.

_____, and _____. 2001. *Taking Center Stage: Masterful Public Speaking Using Acting Skills You Never Knew You Had*. New York: Berkley.

Grant-Williams, Renee. 2002. *Voice Power: Using Your Voice to Captivate, Persuade, and Command Attention*. New York: AMACOM.

Griffin, Emory A. 2000. *A First Look at Communication Theory*. New York: McGraw-Hill.

Hage, Christine Lind, and Stephen Sottong. 2000. Should Libraries Jump on the E-Book Bandwagon? *American Libraries* 31 (7):61–64.

Hall, Danelle. 2002. The Care and Feeding of Speakers and the Spoken-To. *American Libraries* 33 (5):64–65.

Harding, Les. 1994. *A Book in Hand Is Worth Two in the Library: Quotations on Books and Librarianship*. Jefferson, North Carolina: McFarland & Company.

*Hare, A. Paul, Herbert H. Blumberg, Martin F. Davies, and M. Valerie Kent, eds. 1996. *Small Groups: An Introduction*. Westport, Connecticut: Praeger.

Hargie, Owen. 1986. *A Handbook of Communication Skills*. New York: New York University Press.

_____, Christine Saunders, and David Dickson. 1994. *Social Skills in Interpersonal Communication*. 3rd ed. London and New York: Routledge.

*Hartley, James, and Ivor K. Davies. 1978. Note-Taking: A Critical Review. *PLET* 15.

Haynes, Marion E. 1997. *Effective Meeting Skills: A Practical Guide for More Productive Meetings, Crisp 50-Minute*. Menlo Park, California: Crisp Publications, Inc.

Holmes, Nigel. 1984. *Designer's Guide to Creating Charts & Diagrams*. New York: Watson-Guptill Publications.

Ingram, Jay. 1992. *Talk Talk Talk: Decoding the Mysteries of Speech*. New York and London: Anchor Books.

Jackson, Michael Gordon. 2000. Image and Status: Academic Librarians and the New Professionalism. *Advances in Librarianship* 23:93–115.

*Johnson, June. 1998. *You Look Great, but How Do You Sound? How to Speak Like a Pro*. Milwaukee, Wisconsin: Management Strategies, Inc.

Johnstone, A.H., and F. Percival. 1976. Attention Breaks in Lectures. *Education in Chemistry* 13:49–50.

Joss, Molly W. 1999. *Looking Good in Presentations*. 3rd ed. New York: Coriolis Group.

Jurow, Susan. 2001. How People Learn: Applying Adult Learning Theory and Learning Styles Models to Training Sessions. In *Staff Development: A Practical Guide*, edited by E. F. Avery, T. Dahlin and D. A. Carver. Chicago and London: American Library Association.

Kennedy, Joyce Lain. 2000. *Job Interviews for Dummies*. 2nd ed. Foster City CA: FDG Books Worldwide.

Kenny, Peter. 1982. *A Handbook of Public Speaking for Scientists and Engineers*. Bristol and Philadelphia: Institute of Physics Publishing.

Kentie, Peter. 2002. *Web Design Tools and Techniques*. 2nd ed. Berkeley CA: Peachpit Press.

*Klob, Priscilla. *First Impressions, Lasting Impressions: Tips for Job Interviews* [website] 1997 [cited 15 June 2002]. Available from http://www.ala.org/nmrt/footnotes/interview.html.

Koonce, Richard. 1997. How to Ace a Job Interview. *Training & Development* 51 (3):13.

LaGuardia, Cheryl, Michael Blake, Laura Farwell, Caroline Kent, and Ed Tallent. 1996. *Teaching the New Library: A How-To-Do-It Manual for Planning and Designing Instructional Programs.* Vol. 70, *How-To-Do-It Manuals for Librarians.* New York and London: Neal-Schuman Publishers.

Leadley, Sarah. 1998. Teaching Meetings: Providing a Forum for Learning How to Teach. *Reference Services Review* 26 (3/4): 103–108+.

*Lee, Josephine. 1999. The Great Communicators. *Forbes* 163 (6):26–28.

Leeds, Dorothy. 1991. *Powerspeak.* New York: Berkley Books.

Levi, Daniel. 2001. *Group Dynamics for Teams.* Thousand Oaks and London: Sage Publications.

Lienhard, John. *The Engines of Our Ingenuity* [cited]. Available from www.uh.edu/engines/.

Lowe, Doug. 2001. *PowerPoint 2002 For Dummies.* New York: Hungry Minds.

Lucas, Stephen E. 1998. *The Art of Public Speaking.* 6th ed. Boston: McGraw-Hill.

Lutzker, Marilyn. 1986. A Good Teacher: What to Look For, How to Find It. In *Teaching Librarians to Teach: On-the-Job Training for Bibliographic Instruction Librarians,* edited by A. S. Clark and K. F. Jones. Metuchen, New Jersey: Scarecrow Press.

Maier, Norman R.F. 1963. *Problem-solving Discussions and Conferences: Leadership Methods and Skills.* Edited by K. Davis, *McGraw-Hill Series in Management.* New York: McGraw-Hill.

Manley, Will. 1992. *Unprofessional Behavior: Confessions of a Public Librarian.* Jefferson, North Carolina: McFarland & Company.

_____. 1994. *Uncensored Thoughts: Pot Shots from a Public Librarian.* Jefferson, North Carolina: McFarland & Company.

Mathews, Anne J. 1983. *Communicate!: A Librarian's Guide to Interpersonal Relations.* Chicago: American Library Association.

McCallister, Myrna J., and Thomas H. Patterson. 1992. Effective Meetings. In *Practical Help for New Supervisors,* edited by J. Giesecke. Chicago and London: American Library Association.

McCroskey, James C. 2001. *Introduction to Rhetorical Communication.* 8th ed. Boston: Allyn and Bacon.

*McDaniel, Sarah. *Information Literacy Instruction Listserv.* Association of College and Research Libraries [cited 15 June 2002]. Available from http://bubl.ac.uk/mail/ilild/.

McKeachie, Wilbert J. 1999. *McKeachie's Teaching Tips: Strategies, Research, and Theory for College and University Teachers.* 10th ed. Boston and New York: Houghton Mifflin.

*McLain, Bill. 1999. *Do Fish Drink Water? Puzzling and Improbable Questions and Answers.* New York: Morrow.

_____. 2001. *What Makes Flamingos Pink? A Colorful Collection of Q & A's for the Unquenchably Curious.* New York: HarperCollins.

McManus, Judith A. 1998. *How to Write and Deliver an Effective Speech.* New York: Arco.

McManus, Patrick. 2000. *The Deer on a Bicycle: Excursions into the Writing of Humor.* Spokane, Washington: Eastern Washington University Press.

Mehrabian, Albert. 1972. *Nonverbal Communication.* Chicago and New York: Aldine Atherton.

Menzel, Kent E., and Lori J. Carrell. 1994. The Relationship between Preparation and Performance in Public Speaking. *Communication Education* 43:17–26.

Miner, Margaret, and Hugh Rawson. 2000. *New International Dictionary of Quotations.* New York: Signet, Putnam.

Moody, Janett, Brent Stewart, and Cynthia Bolt-Lee. 2002. Showing the Skilled Business Graduate: Expanding the Tool Kit.

Business Communication Quarterly 65 (1):21–36.

Motley, Michael T. 1988. Taking the Terror Out of Talk. *Psychology Today*: 46–49.

Myers, Isabel Briggs, and Peter B. Myers. 1980. *Gifts Differing: Understanding Personality Type*. Palo Alto, California: Davies-Black Publishing.

Naismith, Rachael, and Joan Stein. 1989. Library Jargon: Student Comprehension of Technical Language Used by Librarians. *College and Research Libraries* 50 (5):543–552.

Nilson, Carolyn. 1990. *Training for Non-Trainers: A Do-It-Yourself Guide for Managers*. New York: American Management Association.

Oberg, Larry R. 1992. The Emergence of the Paraprofessional in Academic Libraries: Perceptions and Realities. *College and Research Libraries* 53:99–112.

_____. 1993. Paraprofessionals and the Future of Librarianship. *Library Mosaics*: 8–10.

*_____, Mark E. Mentges, P.N. McDermott, and Vitoon Harusadangkul. 1992. The Role, Status, and Working Conditions of Paraprofessionals: A National Survey of Academic Libraries. *College and Research Libraries*: 215–237.

*Oberg, Larry R., Mary Kay Schleiter, and Michael Van Houten. 1989. Faculty Perceptions of Librarians at Albion College: Status, Role, Contribution, and Contacts. *College and Research Libraries*: 215–227.

Powerful Telephone Skills: A Quick and Handy Guide for any Manager or Business Owner. 1993. *Career Press Business Desk Reference*. Hawthorne, New Jersey: The Career Press.

Rabb, Margaret Y. 1993. *The Presentation Design Book: Tips, Techniques, and Advice for Creating Effective, Attractive Slides, Overheads, Screen Shows, Multimedia and More*. 2nd ed. Chapel Hill, North Carolina: Ventana Press, Inc.

Radford, Marie L. 1998. Approach or Avoidance? The Role of Nonverbal Communication in the Academic Library User's Decision to Initiate a Reference Encounter. *Library Trends* 46 (4):699–717.

*_____. 2001. Encountering Users, Encountering Images: Communication Theory and the Library Context. *Journal of Education for Library and Information Science* 42 (1):27–41.

*Ream, Richard. 2000. Why Are Manhole Covers Round? Assuring a Proper Fit during the Job Interview Process. *Information Today* 17 (5):26–27.

Rees, Nigel. 1999. *The Cassell Dictionary of Anecdotes*. London: Cassell.

Richardson, Matthew. 1997. *Whose Bright Idea was That? Great Firsts of World History*. New York: Kodansa America.

Robert, Henry M., General, Henry M. Robert, III, William J. Evans, Daniel H. Honemann, and Thomas J. Balch. 2000. *Robert's Rules of Order Newly Revised*. 10th ed. Cambridge, Massachusetts: Perseus Publishing.

Robles, Kimberley, and Neal Wyatt, eds. 1996. *Reference Training in Academic Libraries*. Vol. 24, *CLIP Notes*. Chicago: American Library Association.

*Rodenburg, Patsy. 1993. *The Need for Words: Voice and the Text*. London: Methuen Drama.

*Rodgers, Terry. 1997. *The Library Paraprofessional: Notes from the Underground*. Jefferson, North Carolina: McFarland.

*Rosen, Courtney, ed. 2000. *How to Do (Just About) Everything*. New York: Simon & Schuster.

Ross, Catherine Sheldrick, and Patricia Dewdney. 1989. *Communicating Professionally*. Edited by B. Katz. Vol. 3, *How-To-Do-It Manuals for Libraries*. New York and London: Neal-Schuman Publishers.

Ruben, Brent D. 1998. *Communication and Human Behavior*. 4th ed. Needham Heights, Massachusetts: Allyn & Bacon.

Safire, William, ed. 1992. *Lend Me Your Ears: Great Speeches in History*. New York and London: W.W. Norton and Company.

Sager, Don. 1998. Empowering the Library's Support Staff. *Public Libraries*: 33–38.

*Saunders, N.M.M. 2001. Great Speeches:

Recognizing and Honoring Heroes. *Harvard Management Communication Letter* 4 (4):6–8.

Scherdin, Mary Jane. 1994. Myers-Briggs Profiles for Librarians. In *The Whole Library Handbook 3*, edited by G. M. Eberhart. Chicago: American Library Association.

Schwartz, Bernard. 1997. *A Book of Legal Lists: The Best and Worst in American Law*. Oxford and New York: Oxford University Press.

Shannon, Claude E., and Warren Weaver. 1949. *The Mathematical Theory of Communication*. Urbana, Illinois: University of Illinois Press.

Sjodin, Terri L. 2001. *New Sales Speak: The 9 Biggest Sales Presentations Mistakes and How to Avoid Them*. New York: John Wiley and Sons.

*SMART Technologies, Inc. *EffectiveMeetings.com* [website] 2002 [cited 15 June 2002]. Available from http://www.effectivemeetings.com/.

Smith, Voncile. 1986. Listening. In *A Handbook of Communication Skills*, edited by O. Hargie. New York: New York University Press.

Spinrad, Leonard, and Thelma Spinrad. 1997. *Speaker's Lifetime Library*. Revised and expanded edition ed. Seacaucus, New Jersey: Prentice Hall.

Stine, Kate, ed. 1995. *The Armchair Detective Book of Lists: A Complete Guide to the Best Mystery, Crime, and Suspense Fiction*. 2nd ed. New York: Otto Penzler Books.

*Stokes, Stephanie. *Library Media and PR* [website] 2002 [cited 15 June 2002]. Available from http://www.ssdesign.com/librarypr/index.html.

Stuttard, Marie. 1997. *The Power of Speech: Effective Techniques for Dynamic Communication*. Hauppauge, New York: Barron's Educational Series, Inc.

Sullivan, Laura A. 1994. Preparing Great Speeches: A 10-Step Approach. *College and Research Libraries* 11:710+.

Sweeney, Richard. 1997. Leadership Skills in the Reengineered Library: Empowerment and Value Added Trend Implications for Library Leaders. *Library Administration & Management* 11 (1):30–41.

Thomas, Robert McG., and Chris Calhoun. 2001. *52 McGs.: The Best Obituaries from Legendary New York Times Writer Robert McG. Thomas Jr*. New York: Scribner.

3M Meeting Management Team, and Jeannine Drew. 1994. *Mastering Meetings: Discovering the Hidden Potential of Effective Business Meetings*. New York and San Francisco: McGraw-Hill.

*Tobias, Cynthia Ulrich. 1995. *The Way We Work: A Practical Approach for Dealing With People on the Job*. Colorado Springs, Colorado: Focus on the Family.

Torricelli, Robert G., ed. 2001. *Quotations for Public Speakers: A Historical, Literary, and Political Anthology*. New Brunswick, New Jersey: Rutgers University Press.

*Tuleja, Tad. 1992. *American History in 100 Nutshells*. New York: Fawcett Columbine.

Turner, Anne M. 1993. *It Comes with the Territory: Handling Problem Situations in the Library*. Jefferson, North Carolina: McFarland & Company.

Useless Knowledge.com 2002. [cited 2002]. Available from www.uselessknowledge.com.

Vonnegut, Kurt. 1981. *Palm Sunday*. New York: Delacorte Press.

Wallechinsky, David. 1995. *The 20th Century: The Definitive Compendium of Astonishing Events, Amazing People, and Strange-but-True Facts*. New York and Boston: Little, Brown and Company.

_____, and Amy Wallace, eds. 1993. *The Book of Lists: The 90s Edition*. Boston and New York: Little, Brown and Company.

*Wanden, Joy A. 2001. Making Meetings Matter! *Library Mosaics* 12 (4):8–12.

Weaver, Maggie. 1999. Reach Out through Technology: Make Your Point with Effective A/V. *Computers in Libraries* 19 (4):62–65.

Weaver-Meyers, Pat L. 2001. Creating Effective Training Programs. In *Staff Development: A Practical Guide*, edited by E. F. Avery, T. Dahlin and D. A. Carver. Chicago and London: American Library Association.

Wilder, Lilyan. 1999. *7 Steps to Fearless Speaking.* New York: Wiley and Sons.

Withers, Carol M. 1995. Being Effective in the Classroom. In *Teaching Electronic Information Literacy: A How-To-Do-It Manual,* edited by D. A. Barclay. New York and London: Neal-Schuman Publishers, Inc.

Wright, John W., ed. 2001. *The New York Times Almanac 2002.* New York: Penguin USA.

*Zahn, David. 1998. Lessons from the Front, Back, and Sides of the Room. *Training & Development* 52 (1):12–13.

*Zielinski, Dave. 2002. How to Make the Most of Your Presentation Preparation Time. *Presentations* 16 (2):32–38.

Index